Share your colored versions with us! We love seeing your results and hearing from you we are social!

The Official FB book page, stay on top of what we have in the works!
www.facebook.com/AMVWART

The Community group, share your colored pages, meet the artists, enjoy exclusive freebies, take part in community Charity books and so much more......
www.facebook.com/groups/fansandfriendsamvwart
www.facebook.com/groups/ColorAWeirdieADay
Follow us on Twitter.... @GlobalDoodlegem
We are on Instagram too
@globaldoodlegems for instagram
...and if you are not social like that we have a blog
globaldoodlegems.wordpress.com

Copyright © 2019 Global Doodle Gems.
All rights are reserved by Global Doodle Gems.
Duplication of pages for personal use are allowed. You are invited to color the pages then scan/post your coloured versions to social networks, mentioning the book title and author/artist (Global Doodle Gems).
All artwork and images are protected by copyright laws. This book or any portion thereof may not, otherwise, be reproduced and/or distributed or transmitted without the express written permission of the artist/publisher of Global Doodle Gems.
All of us from the Global Doodle Gems wish you a colortastic time and look forward to seeing your wonderful color results online!

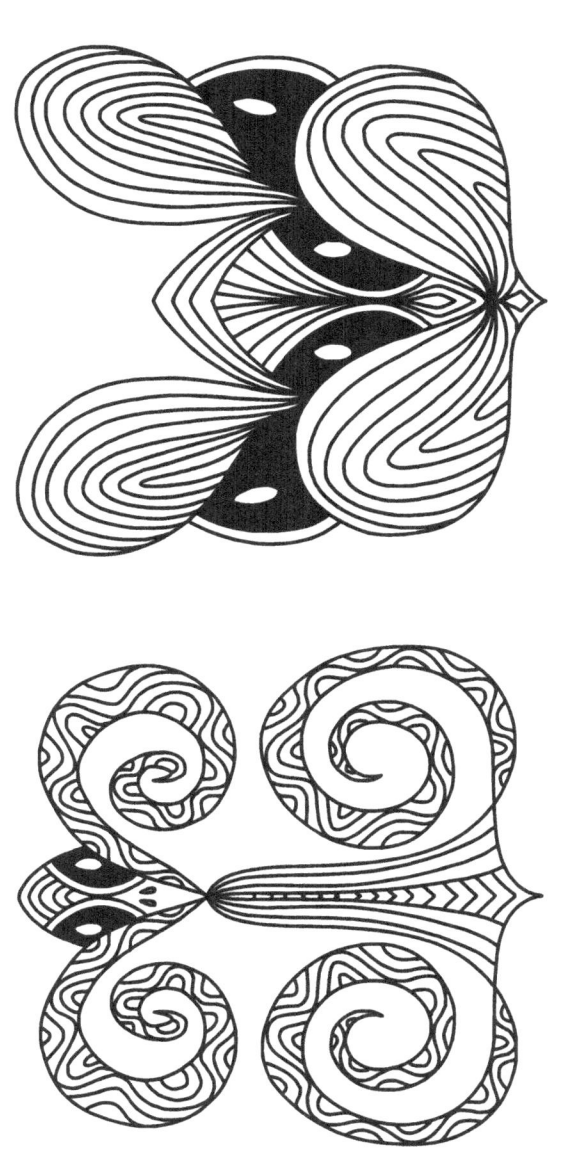

Fatliner Weirdies Volume 1

My first set of Fatliner Weirdies from Fatliner Weirdies The Templates 1

"This book is dedicated to the love of my life, my daughter Victoria Panthera. I make these books in hopes that your life as an adult will be everything you want It to be! I love you more than words can say!"

Maria Wedel

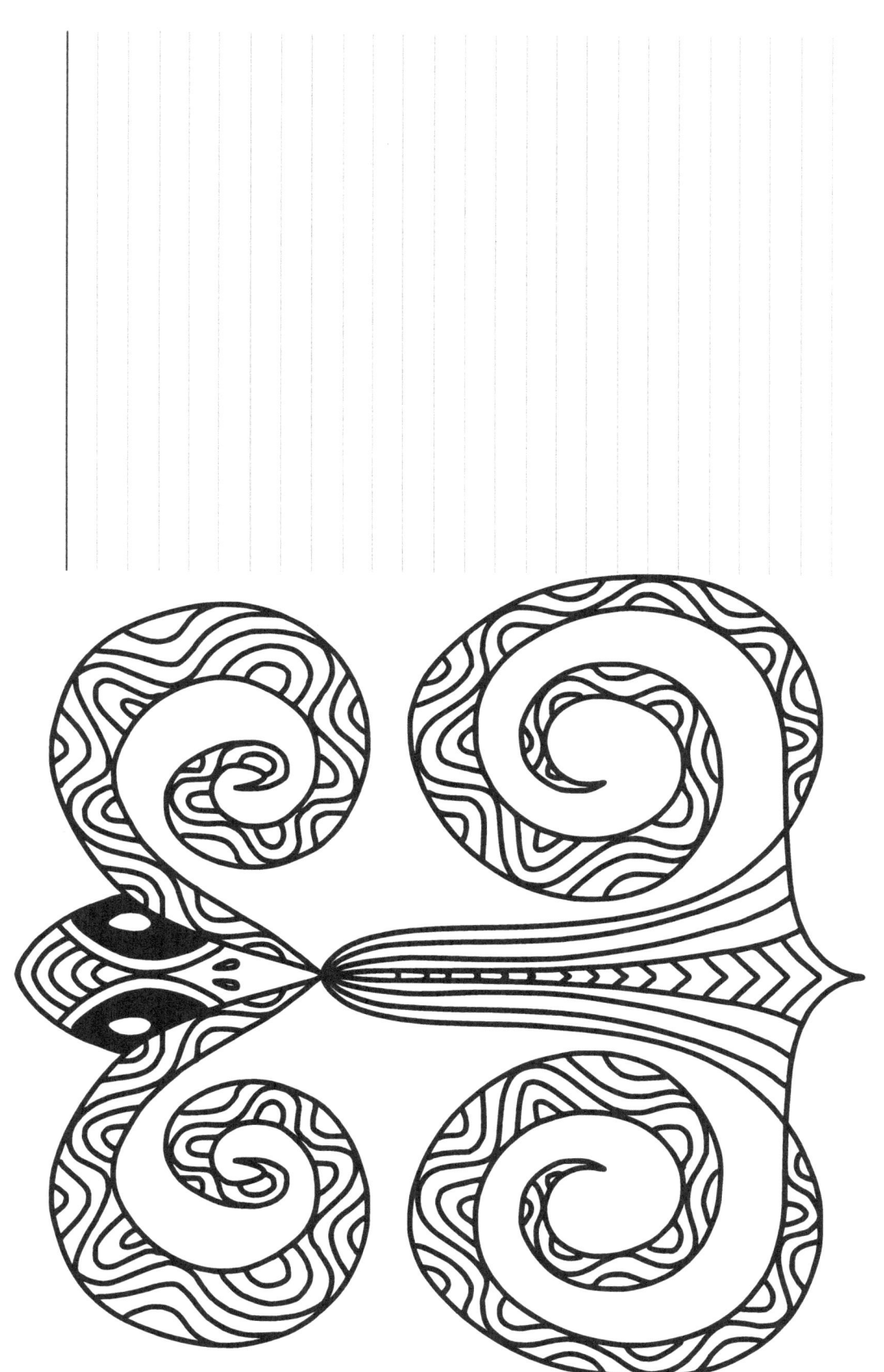

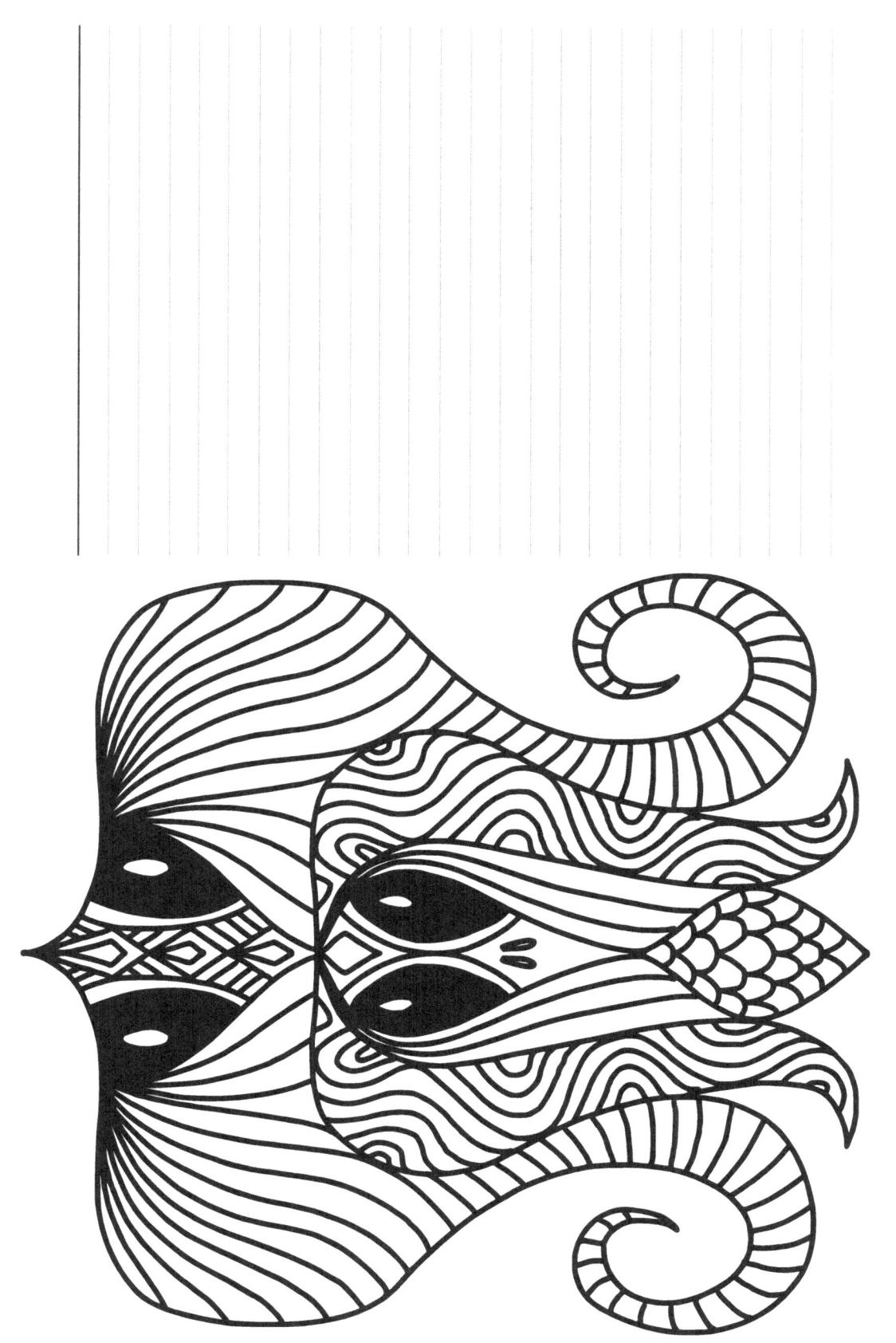

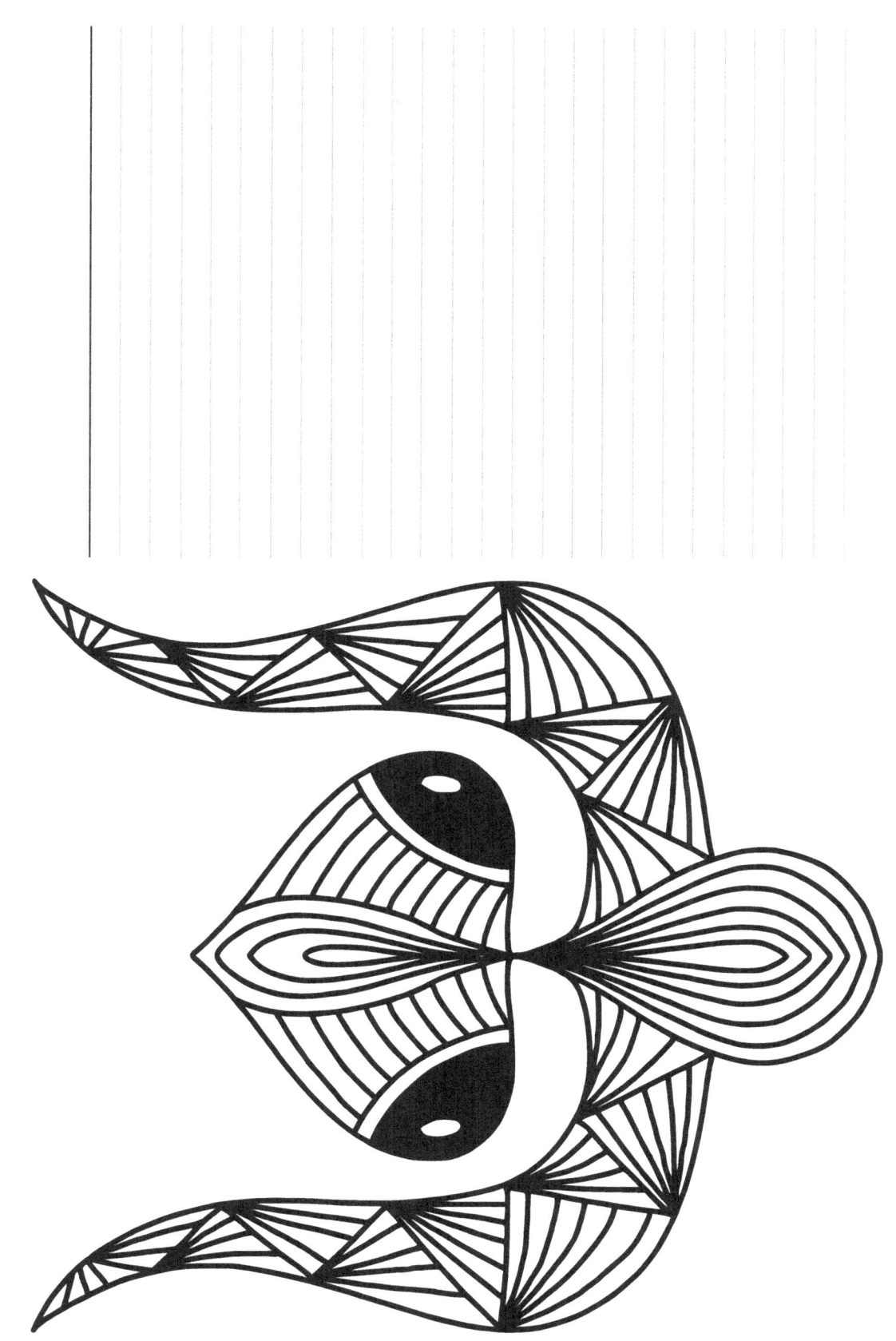

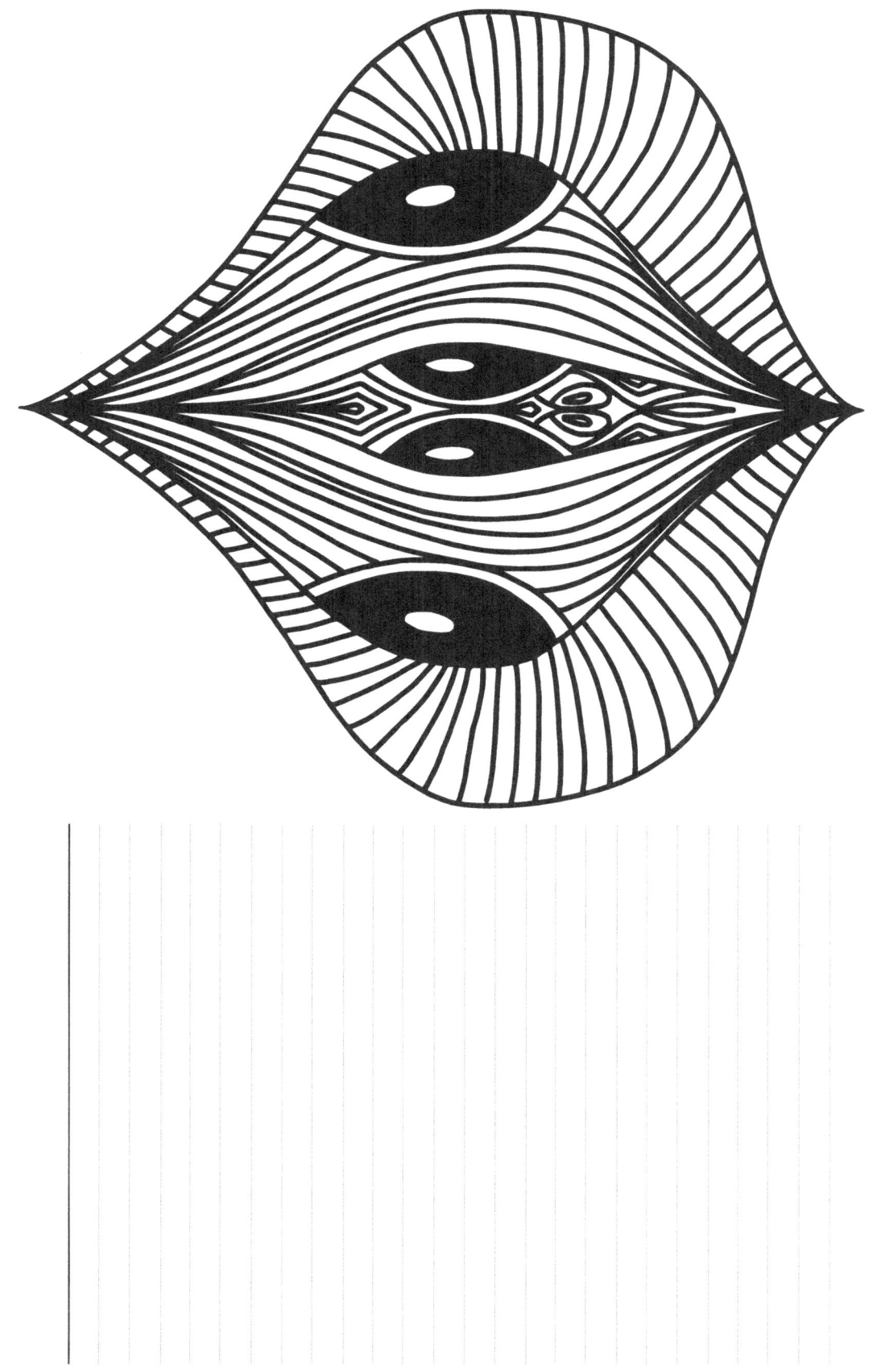

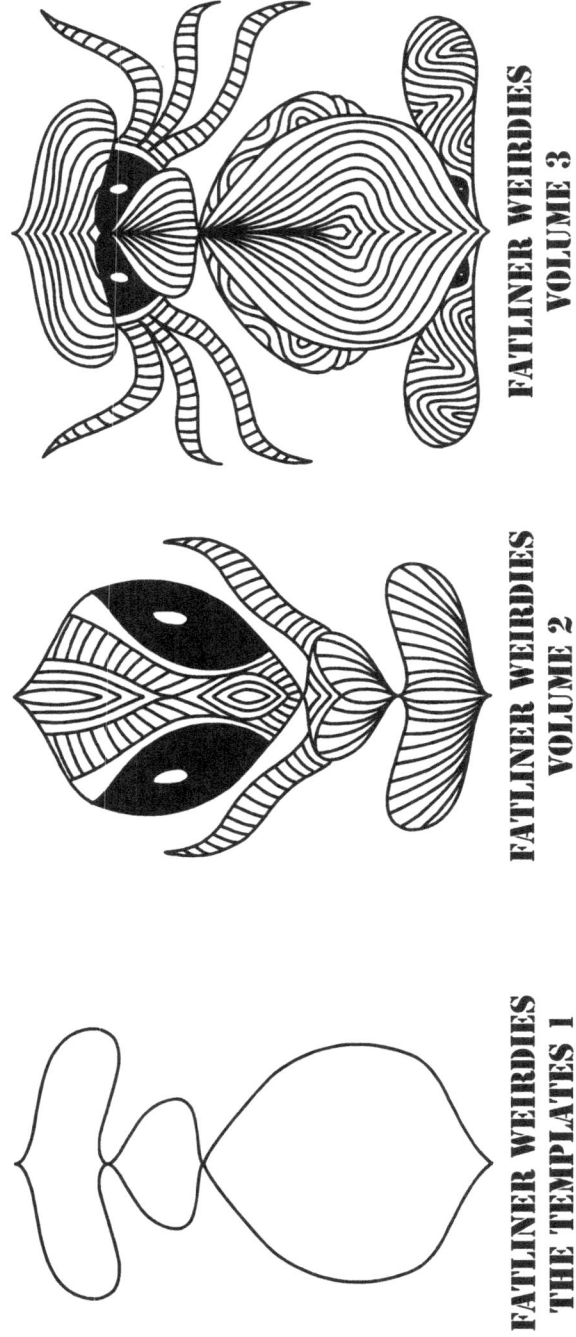

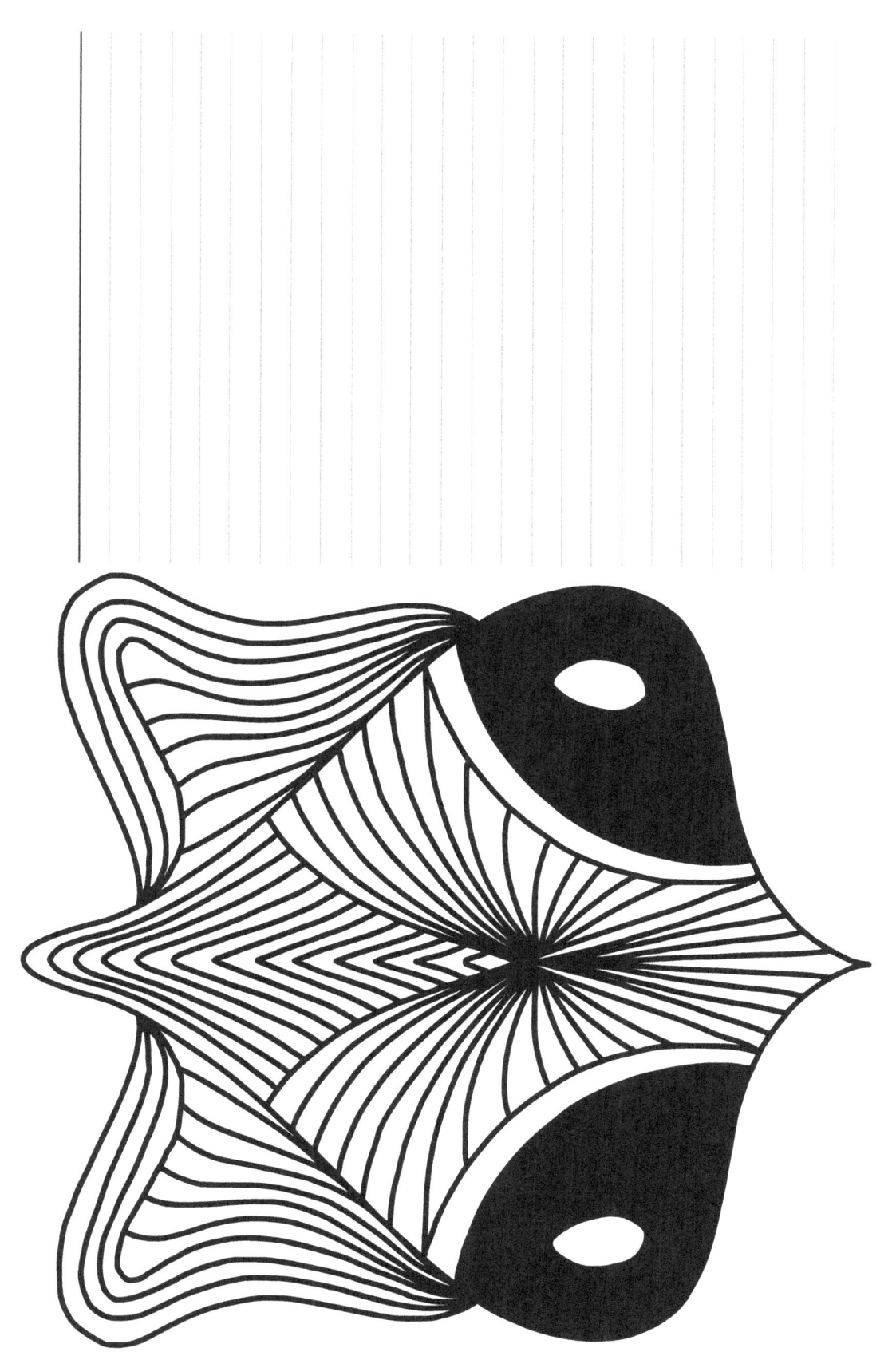

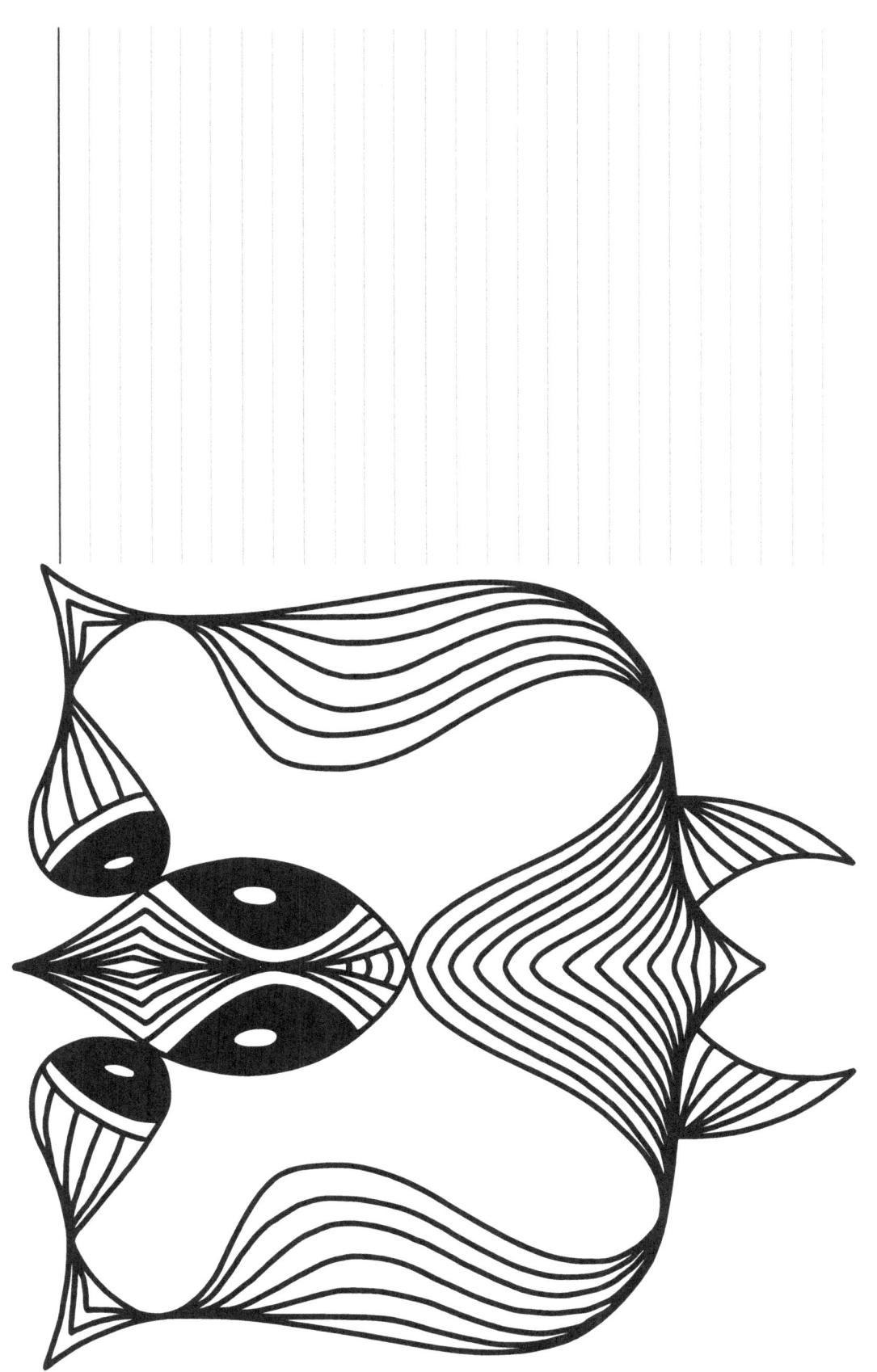

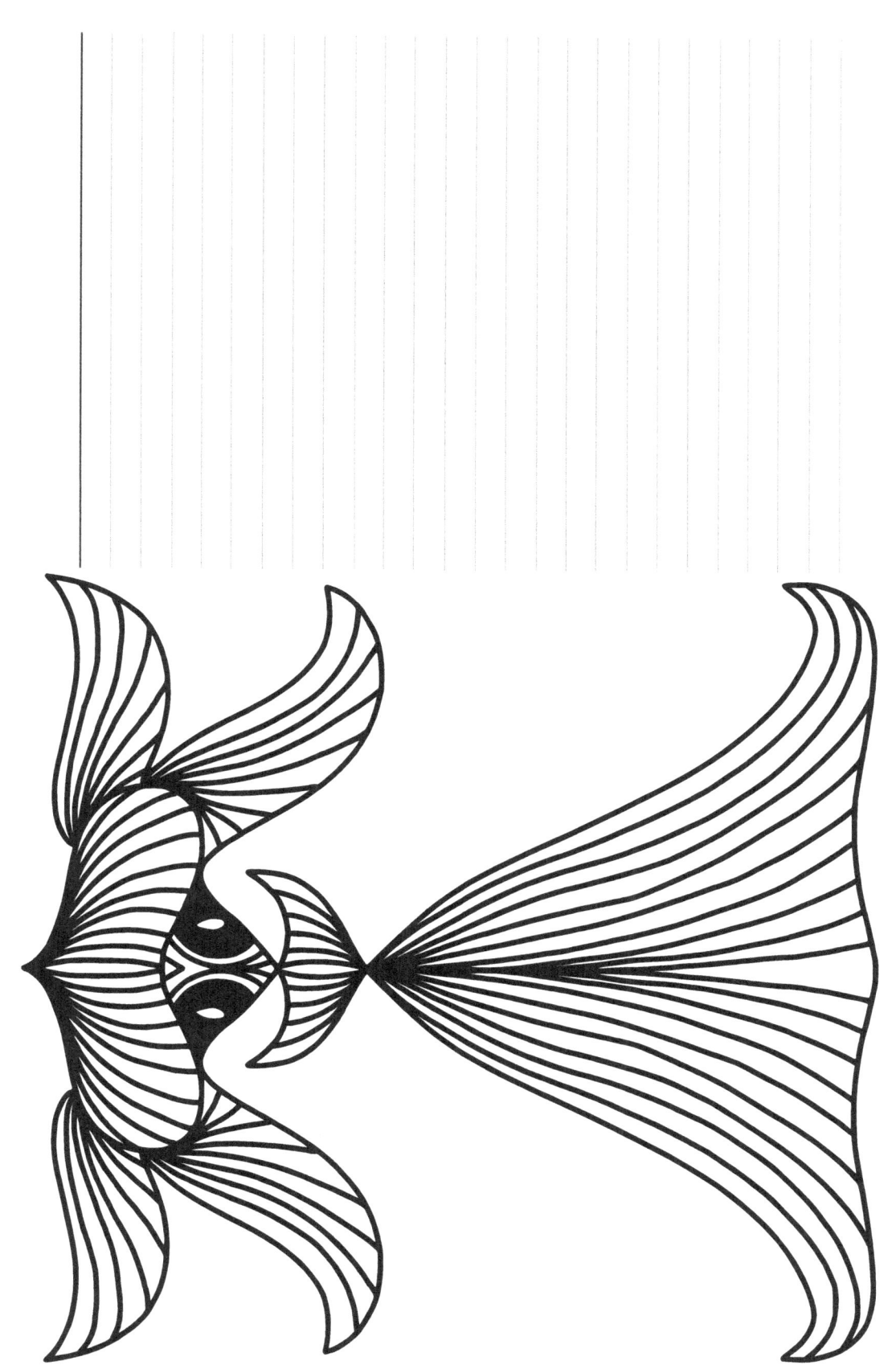

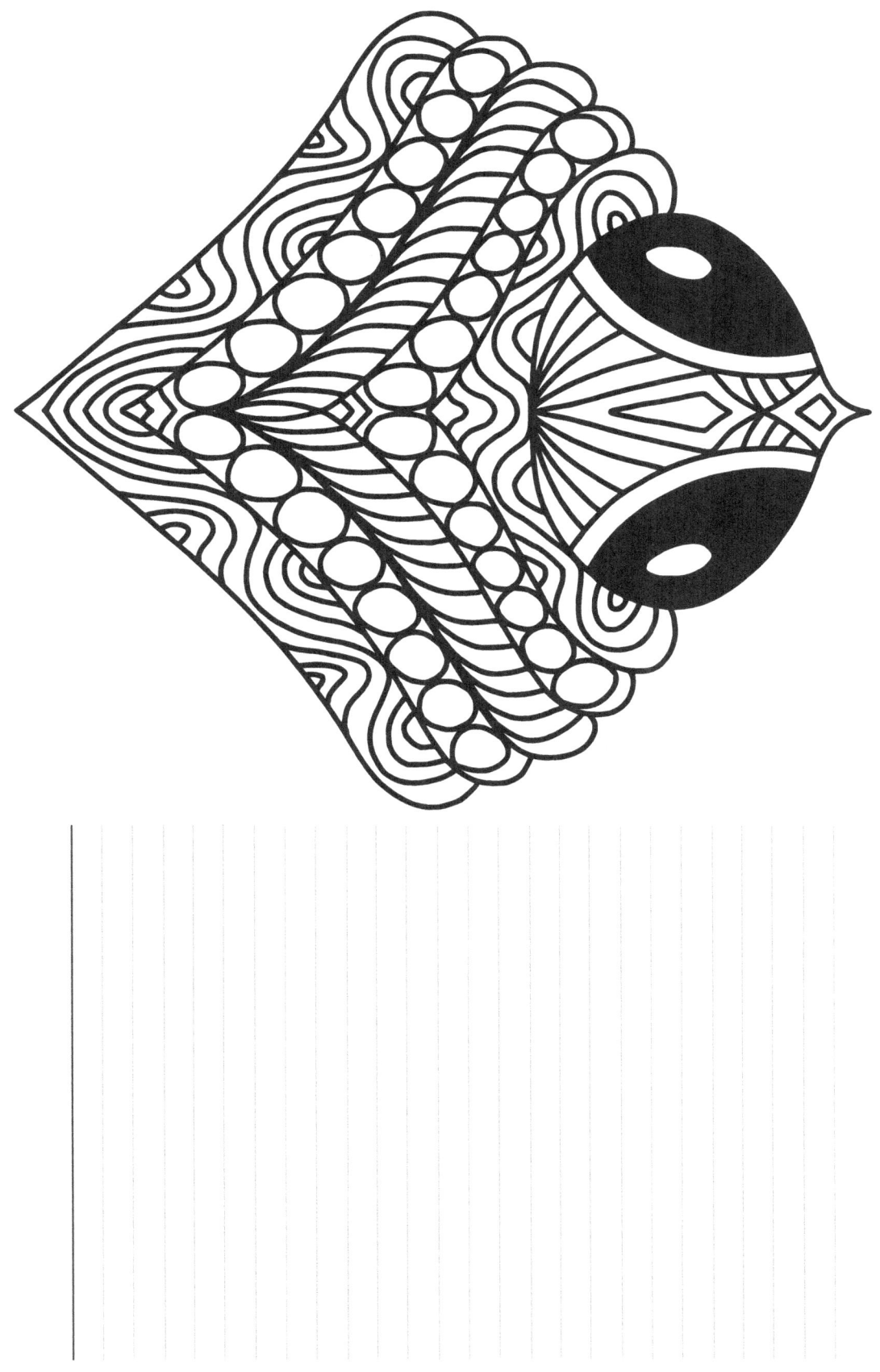

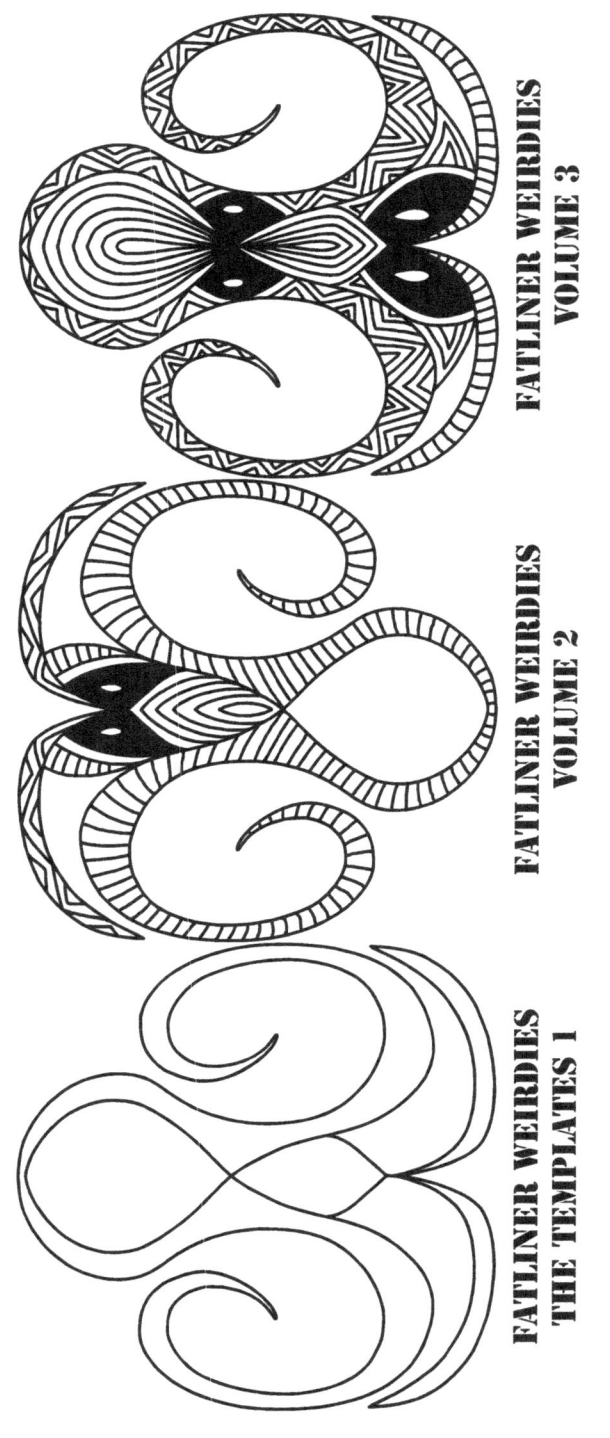

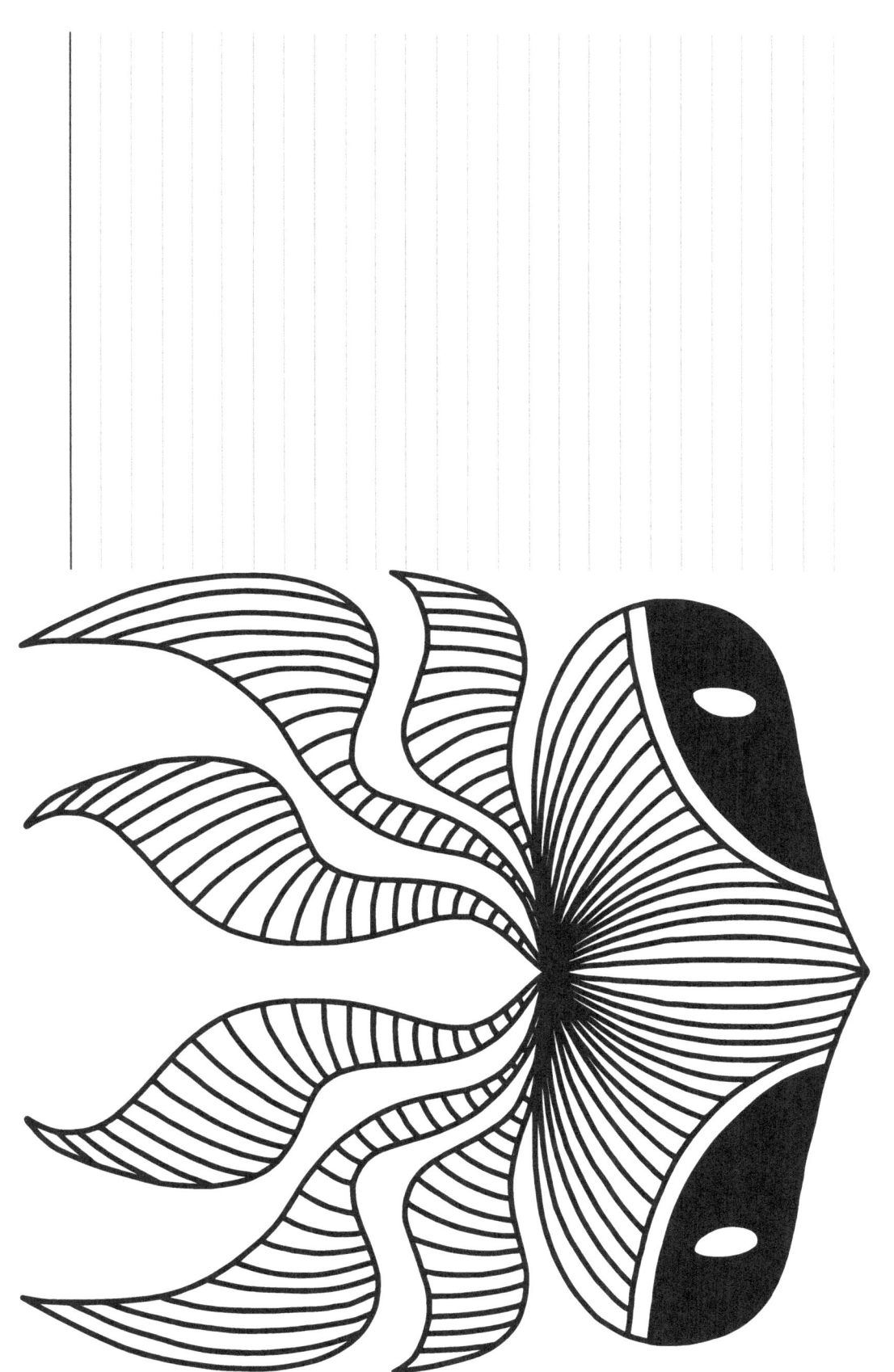

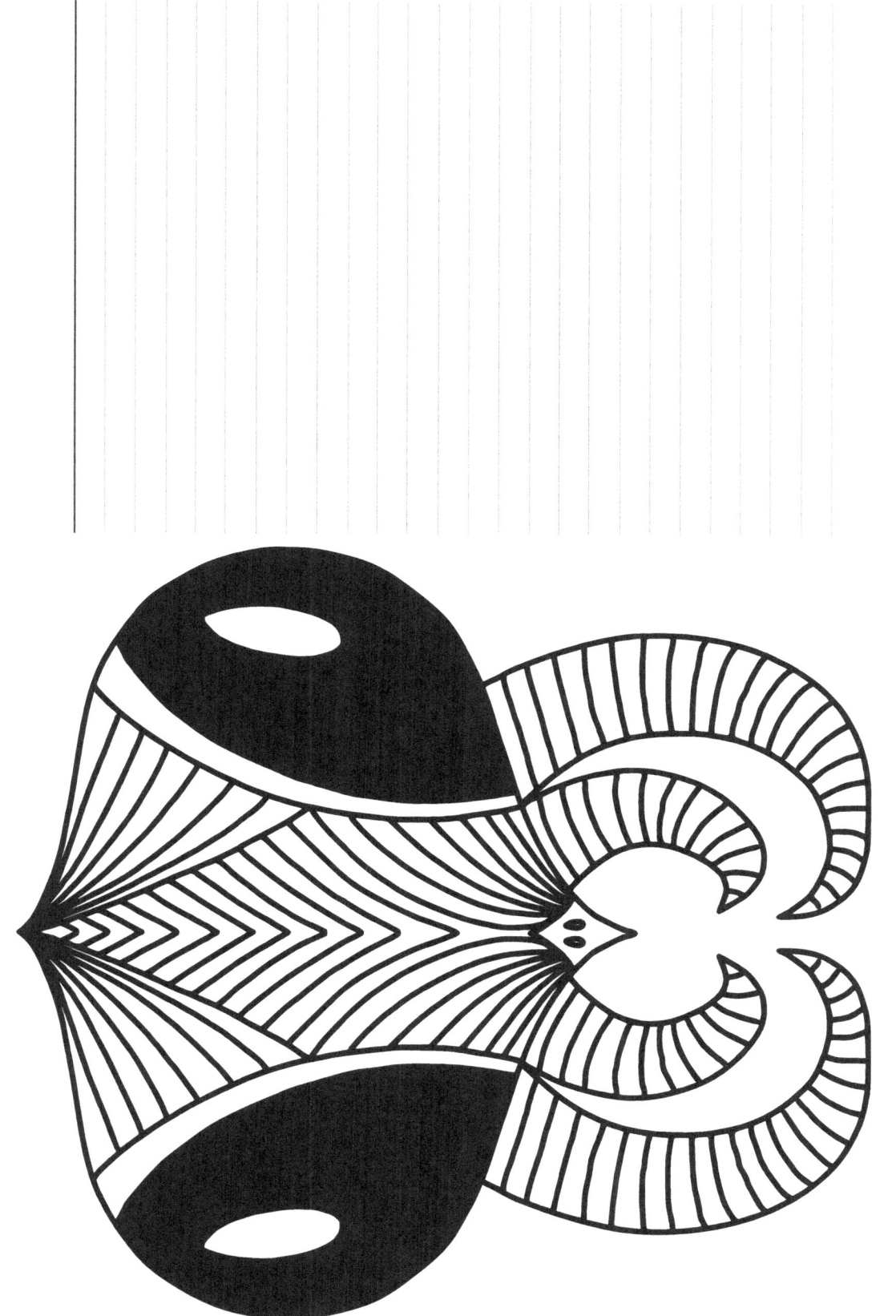

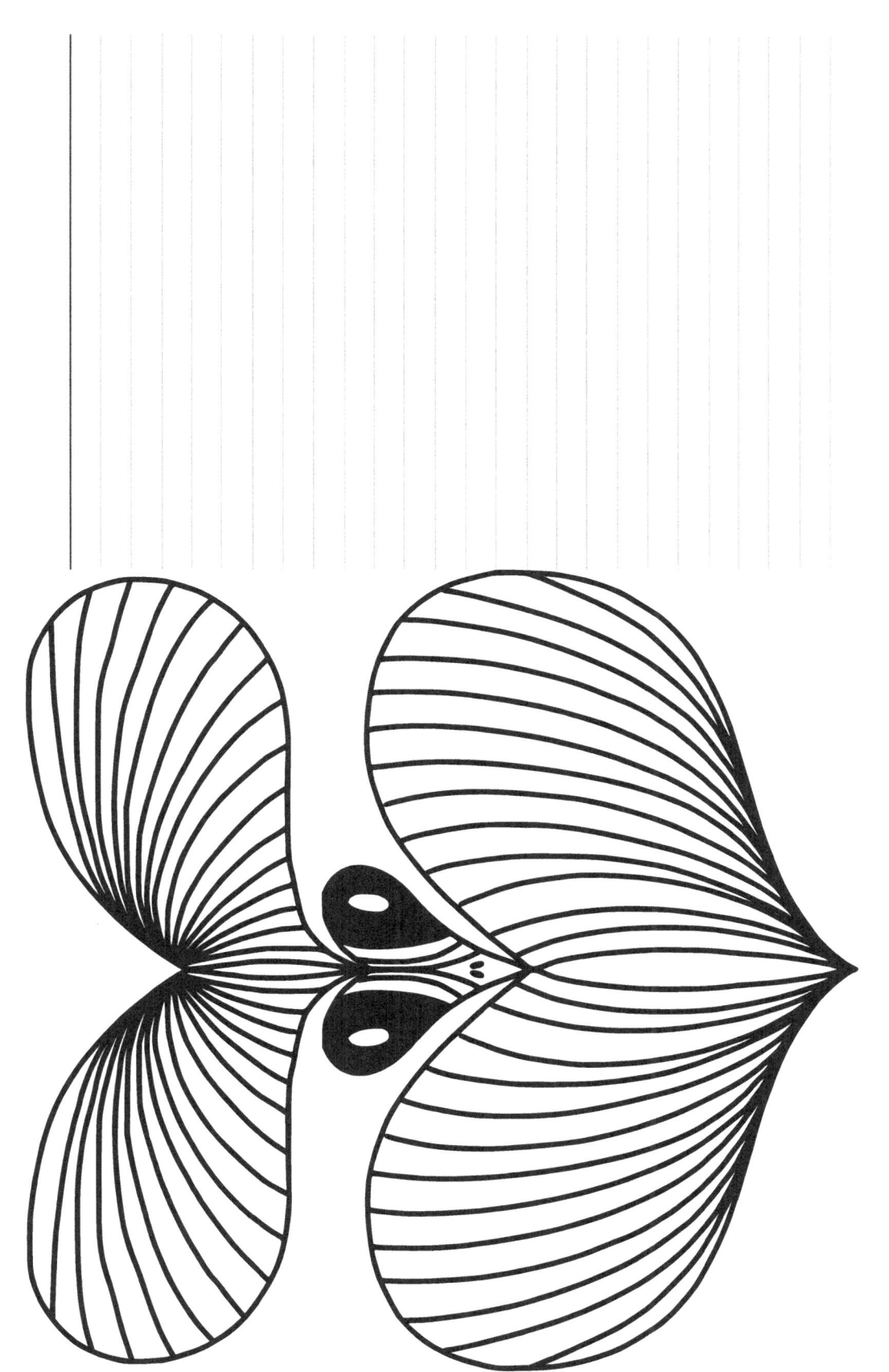

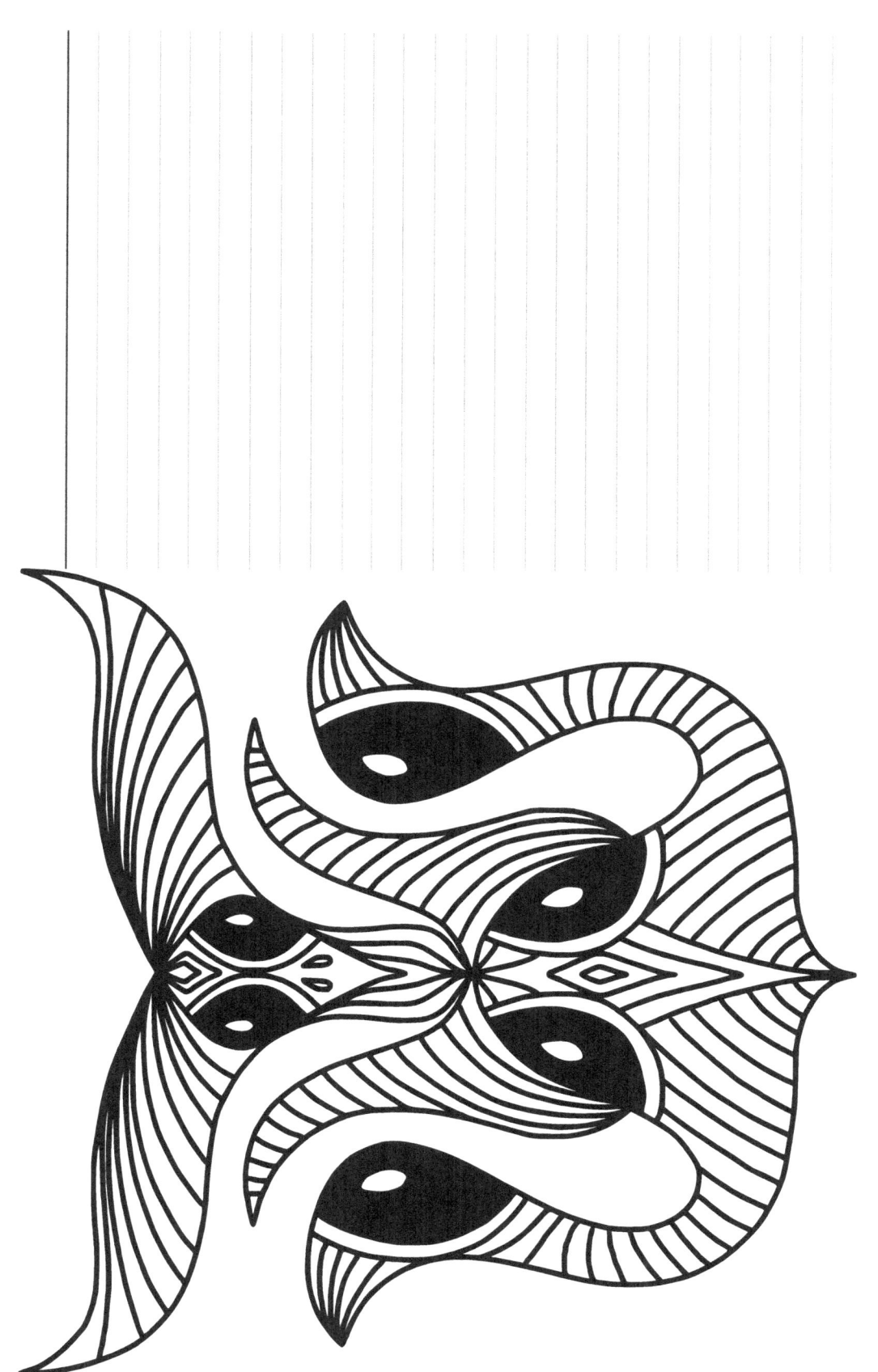

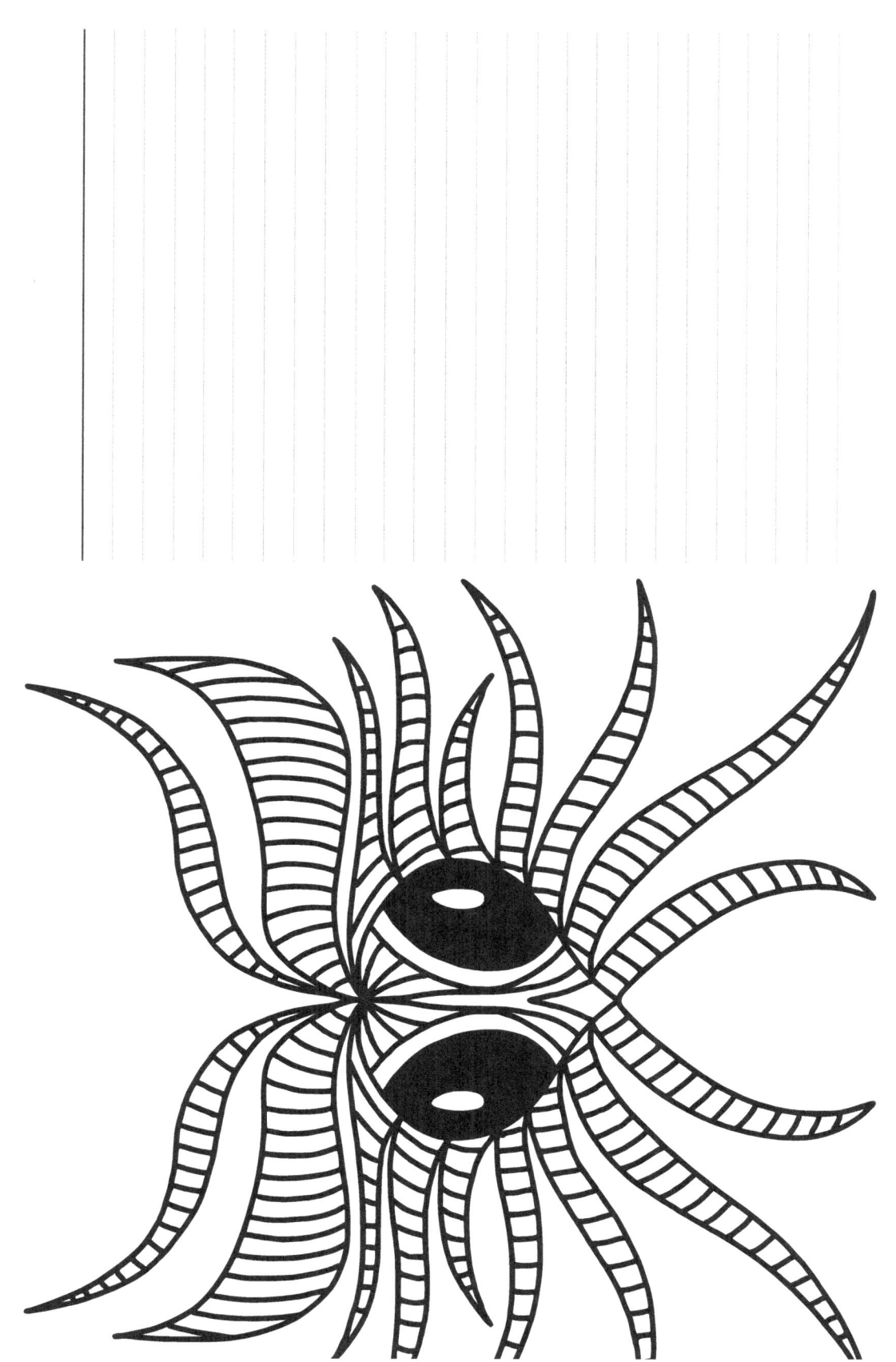

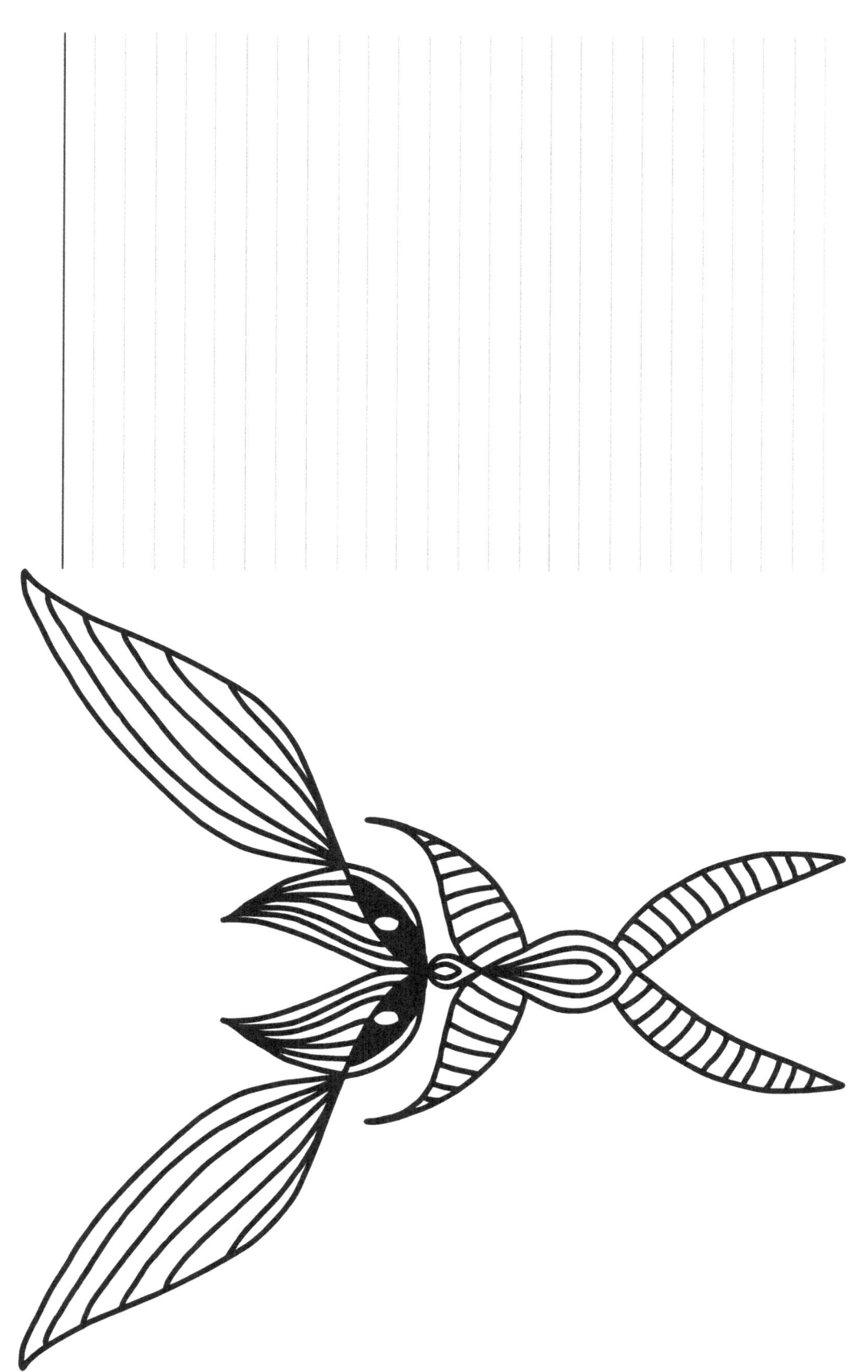

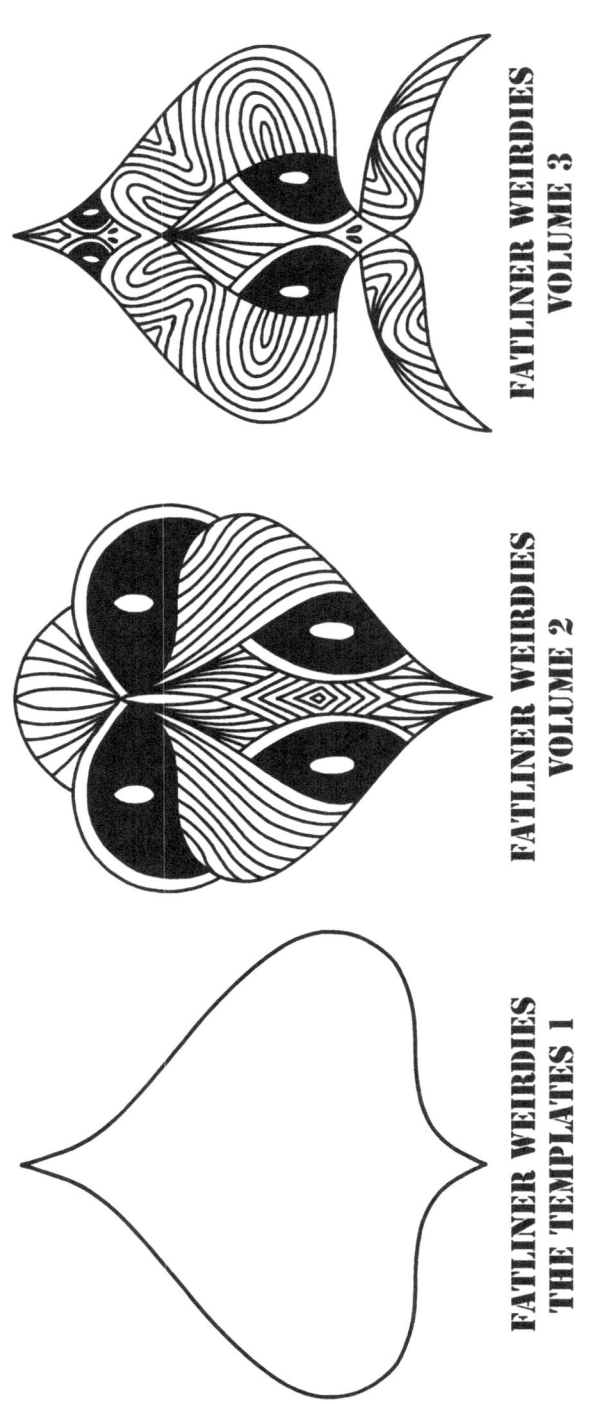

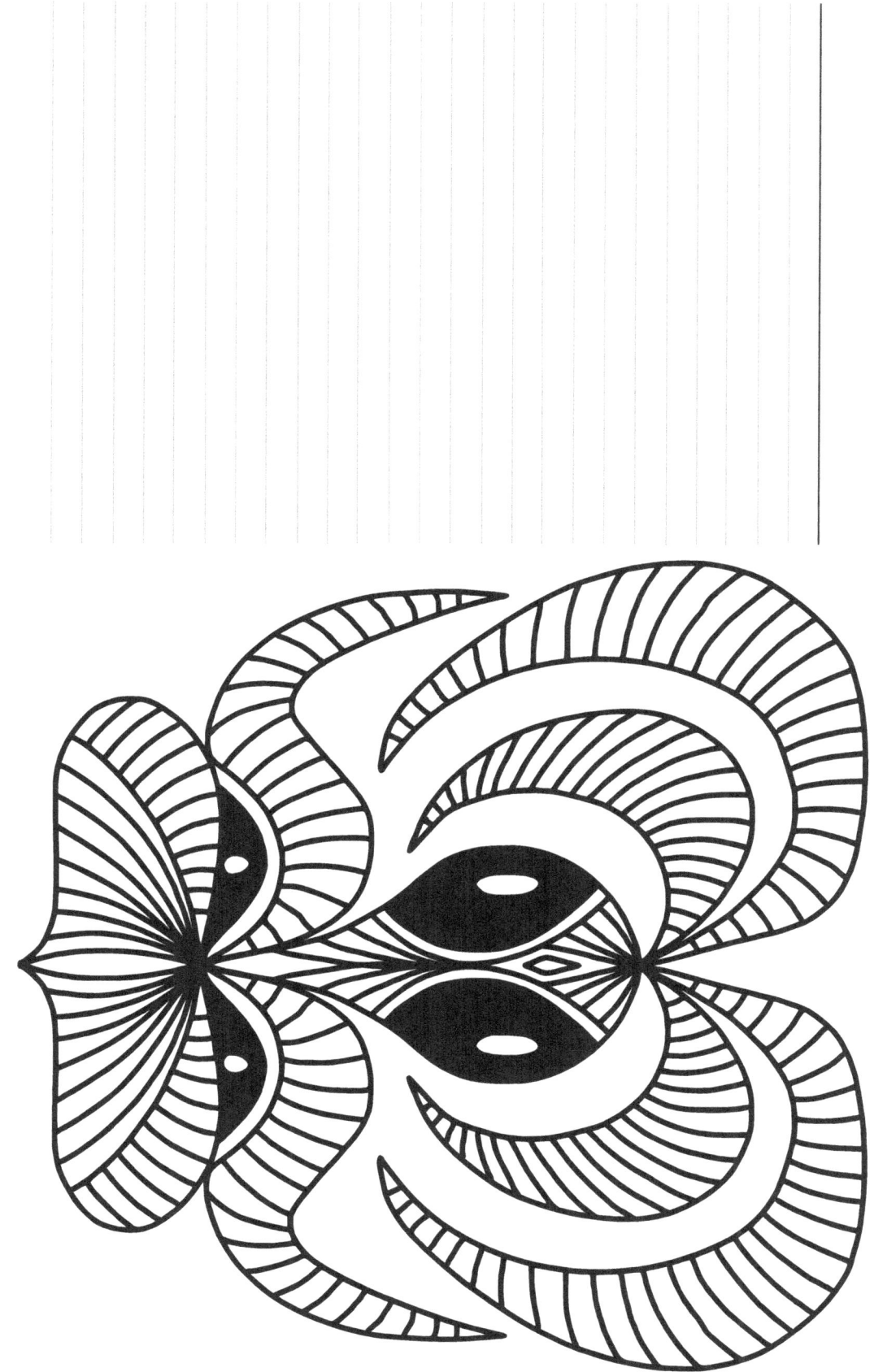

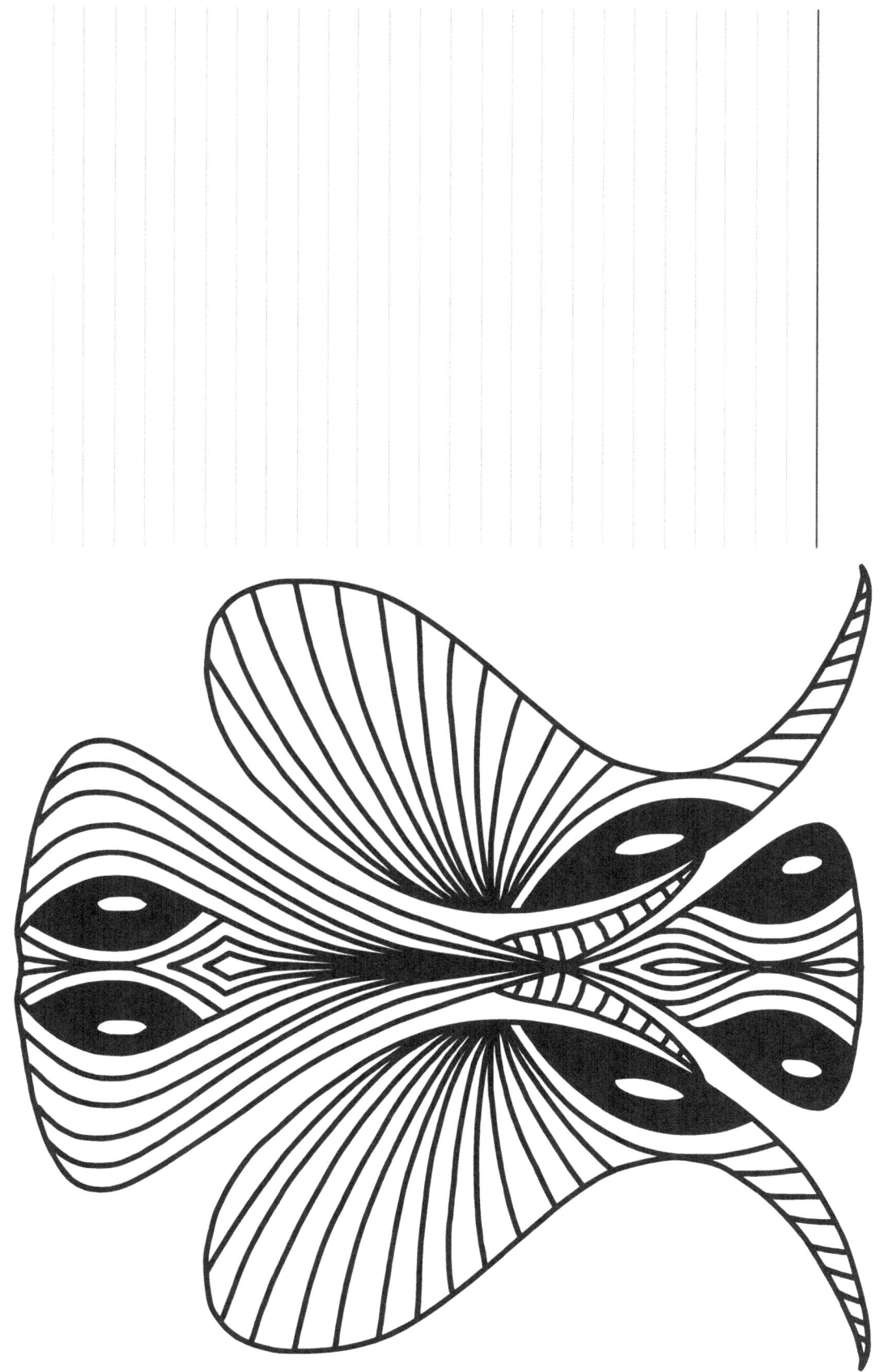

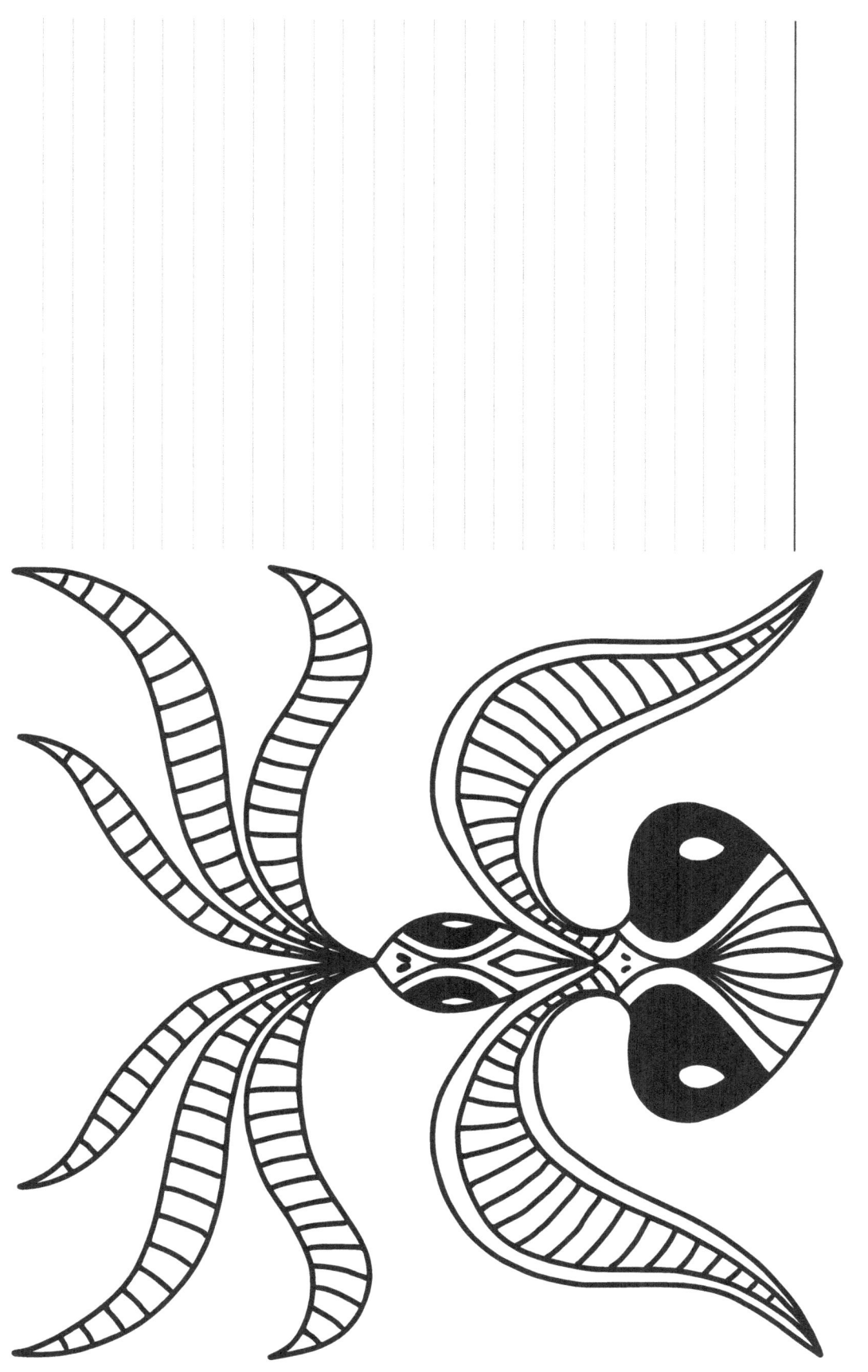

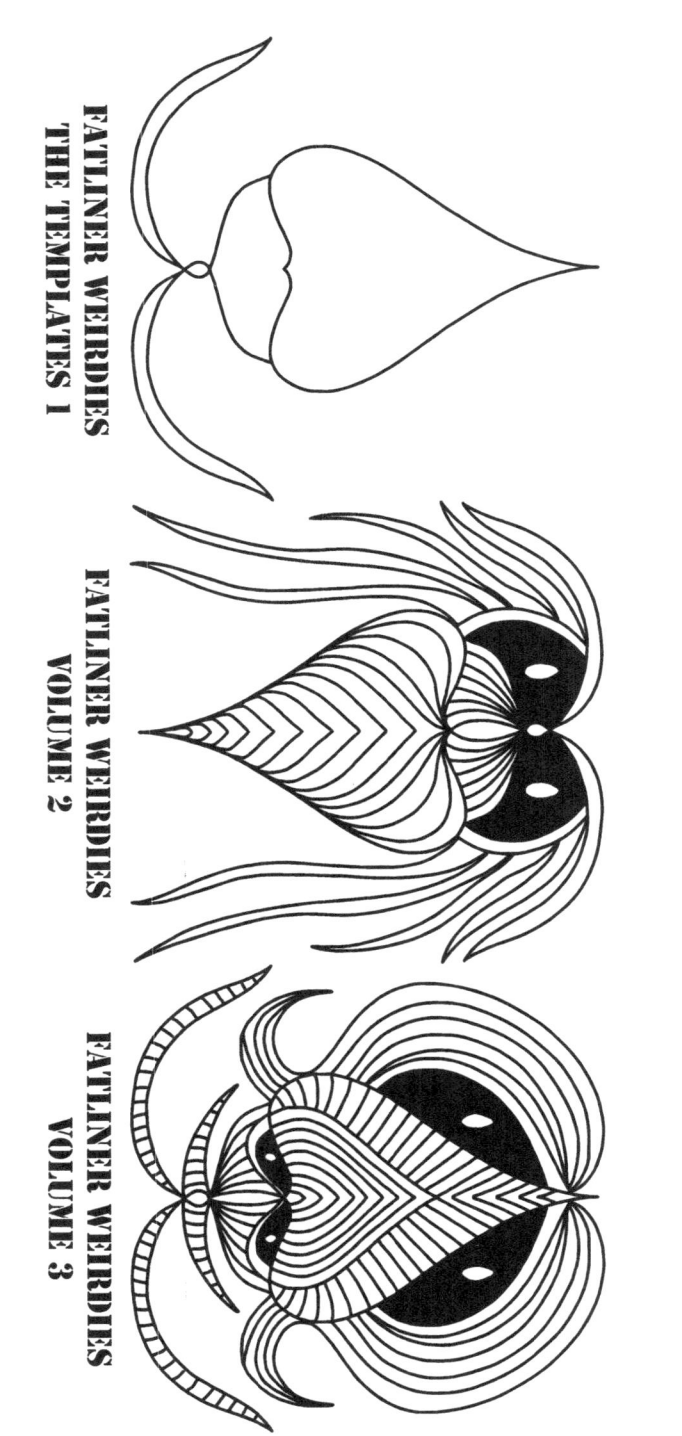

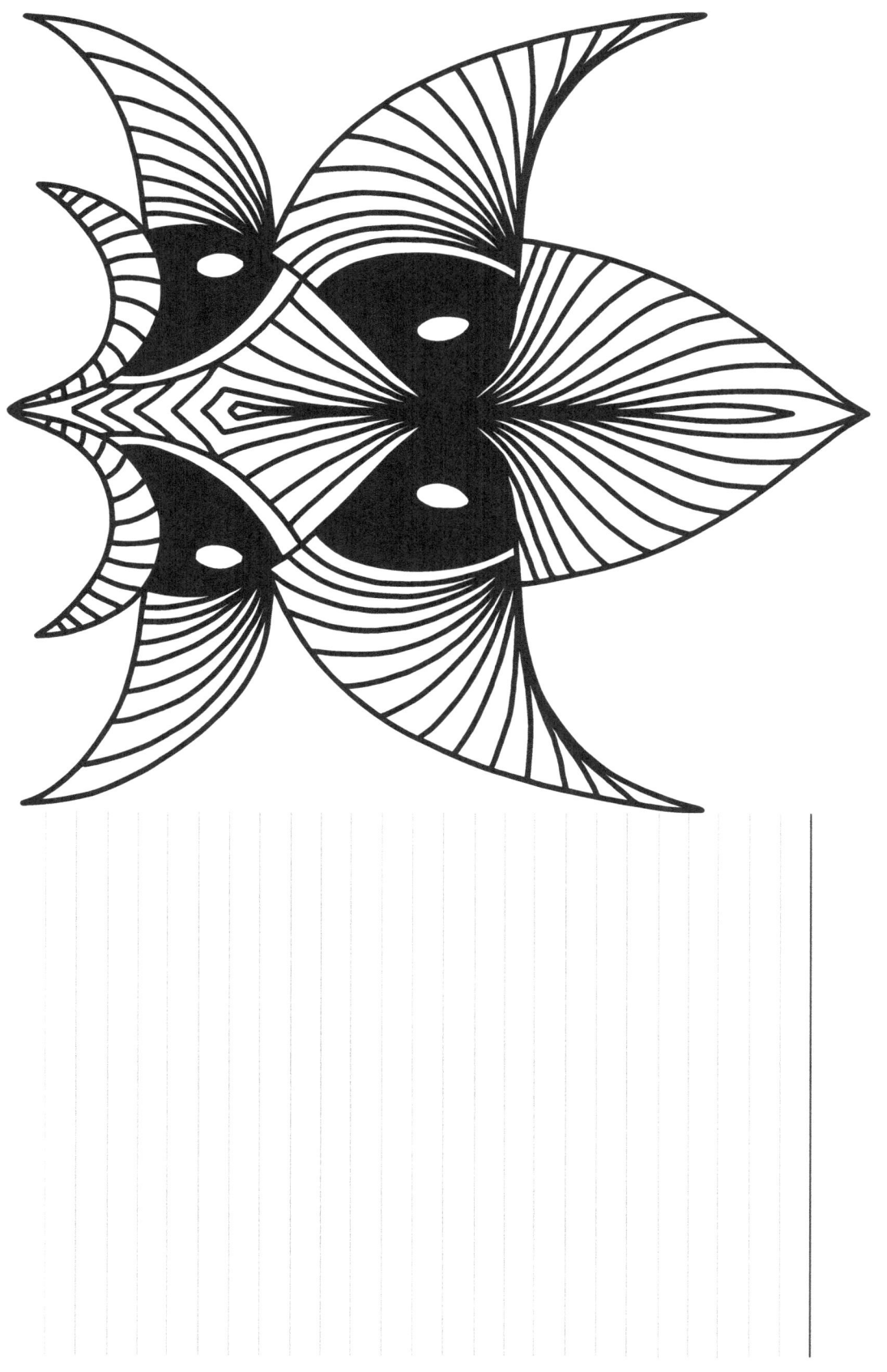

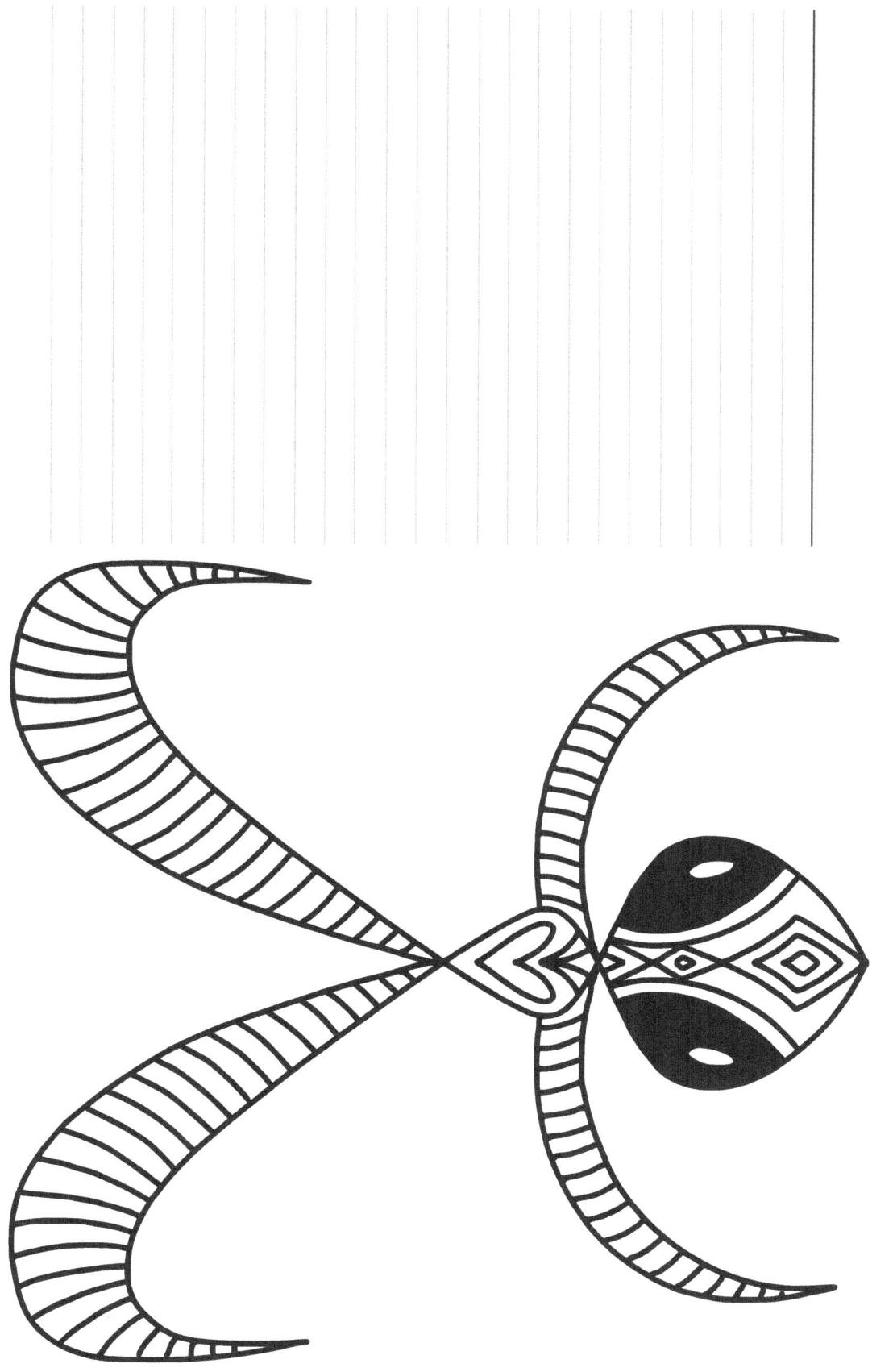

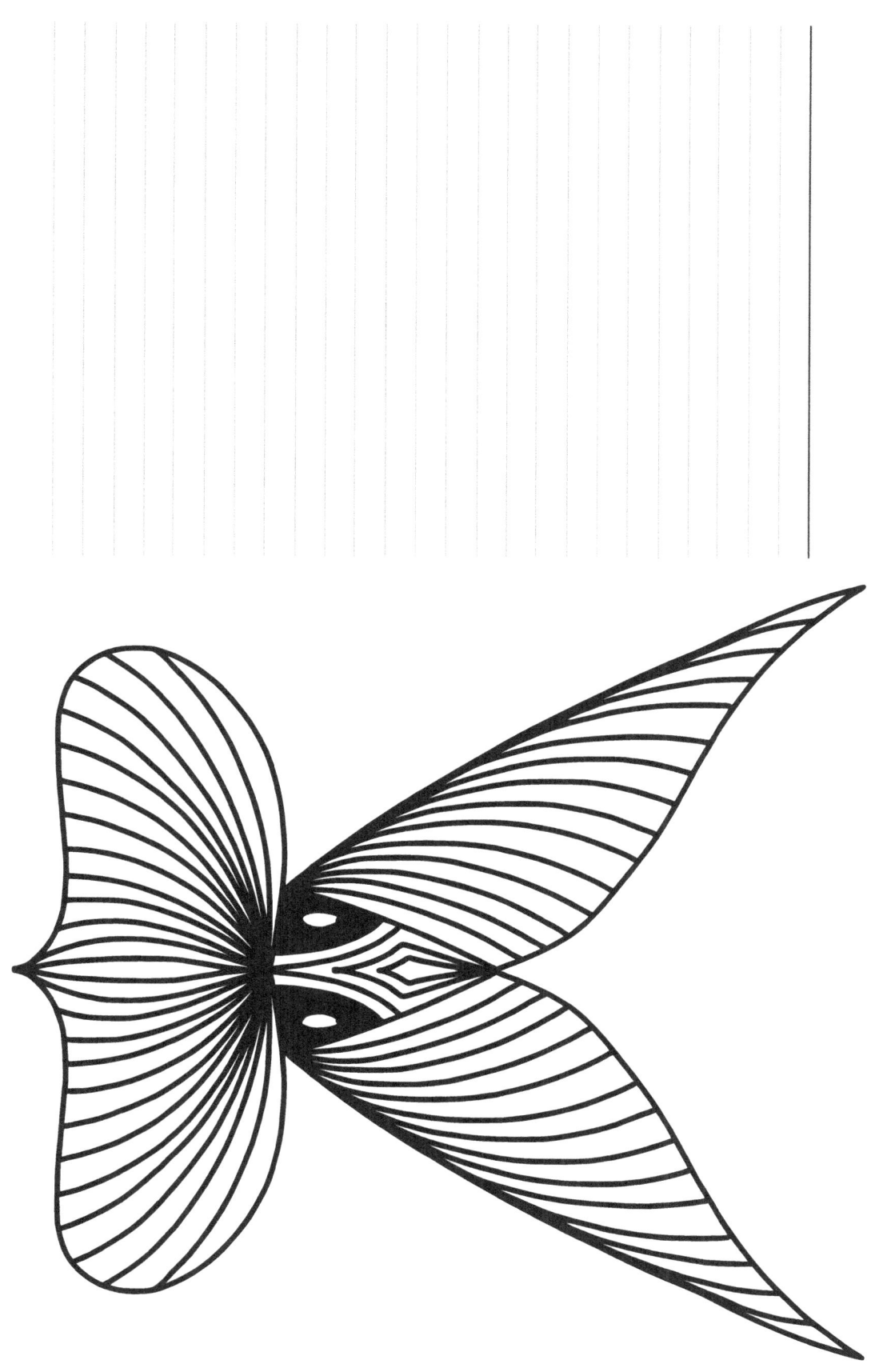

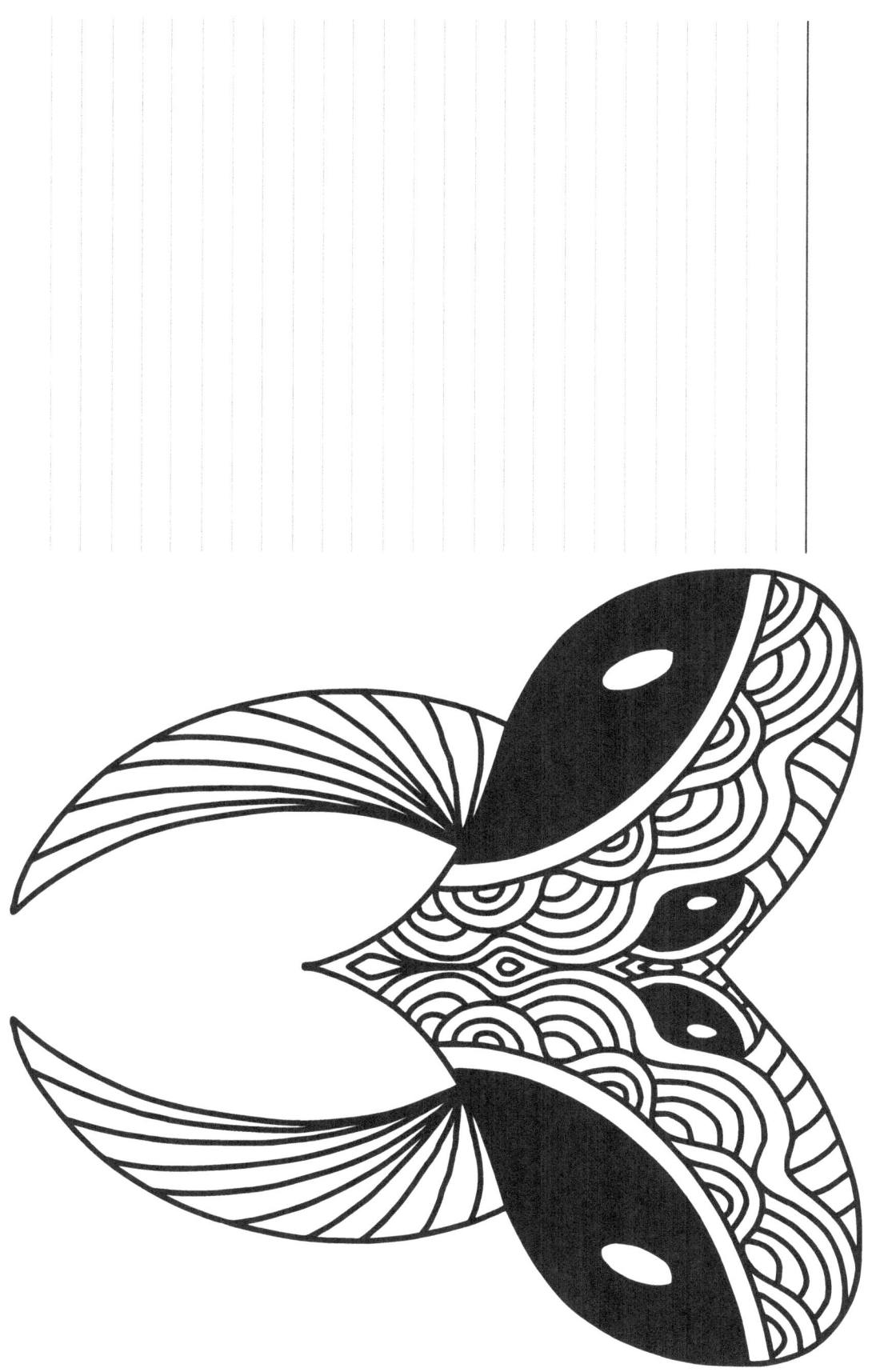

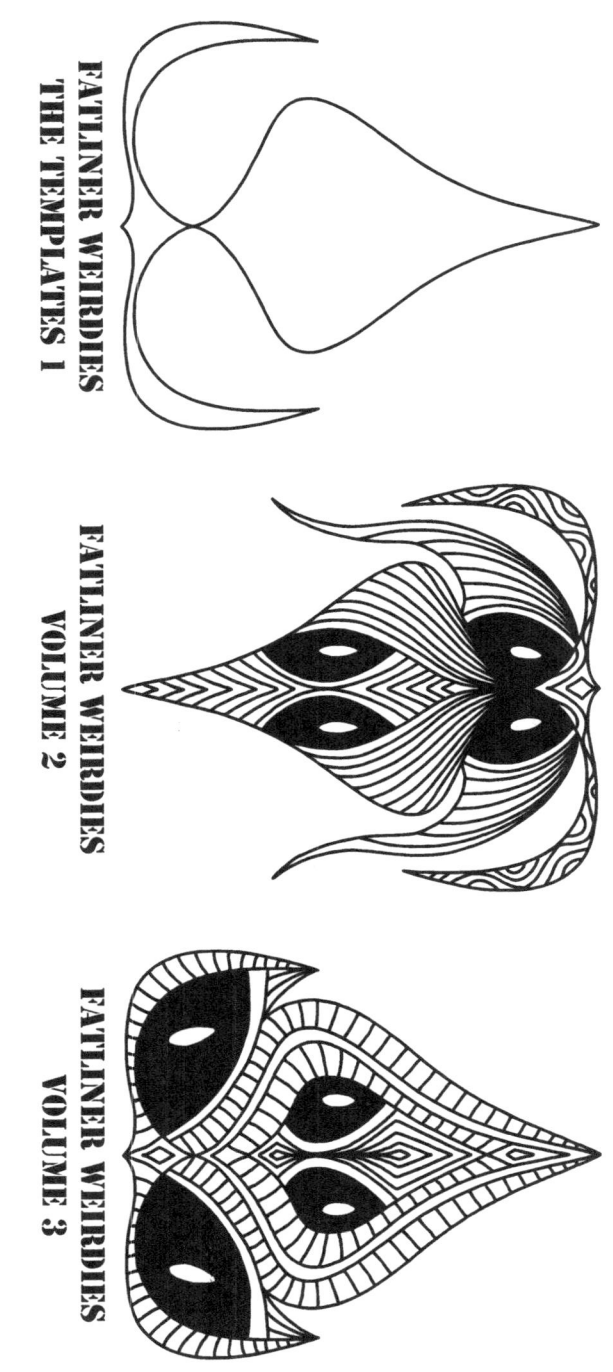

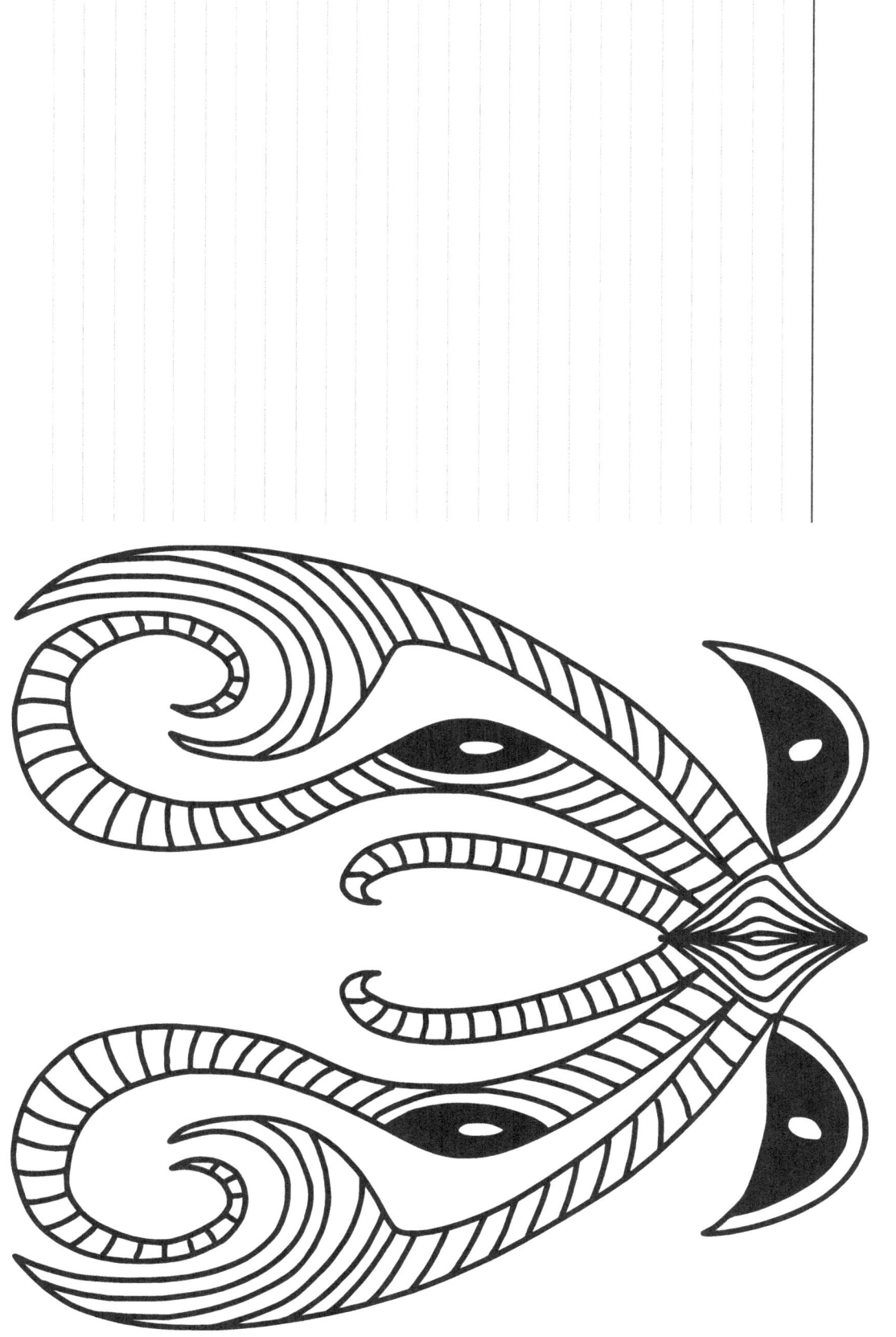

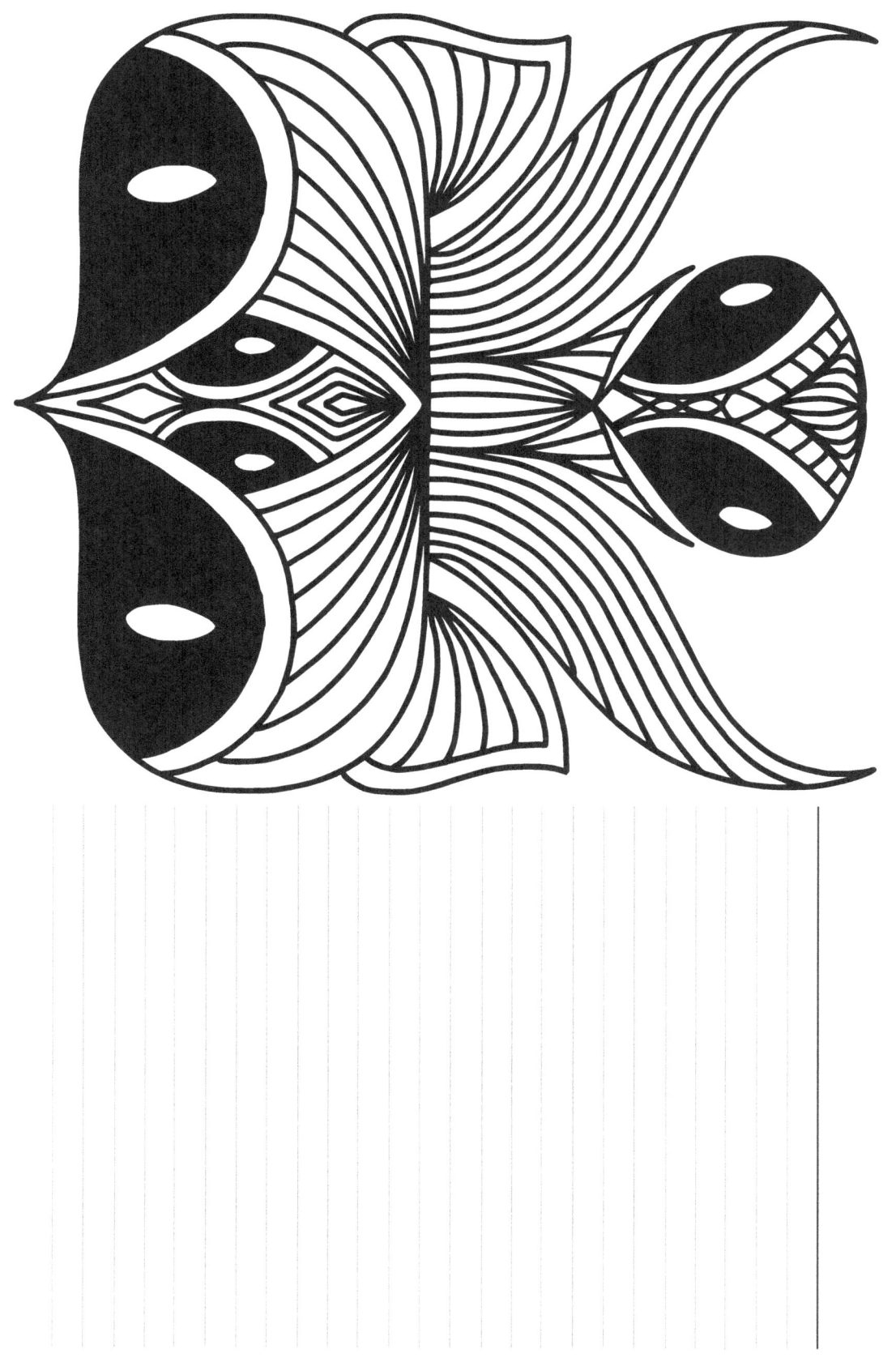

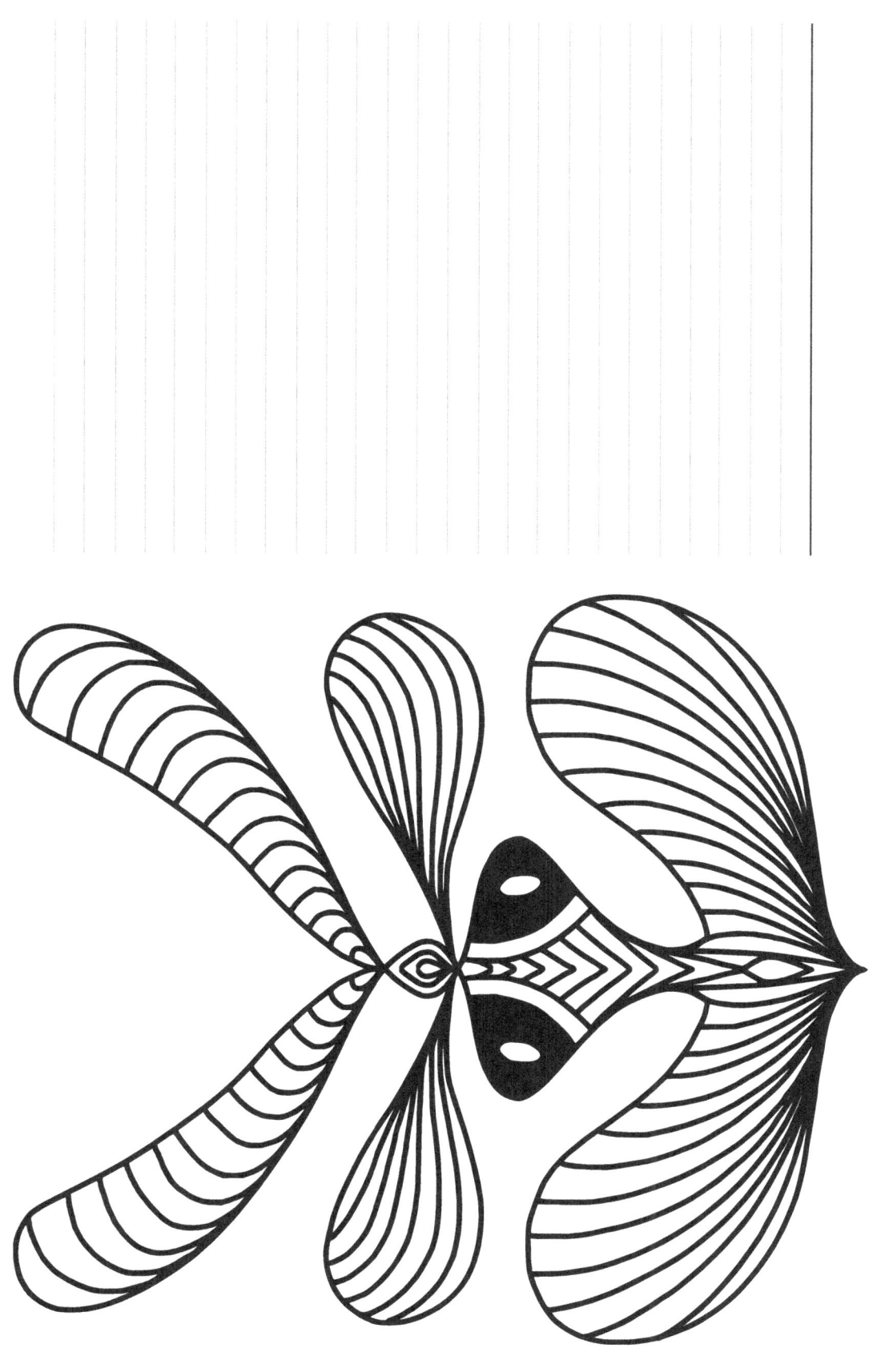

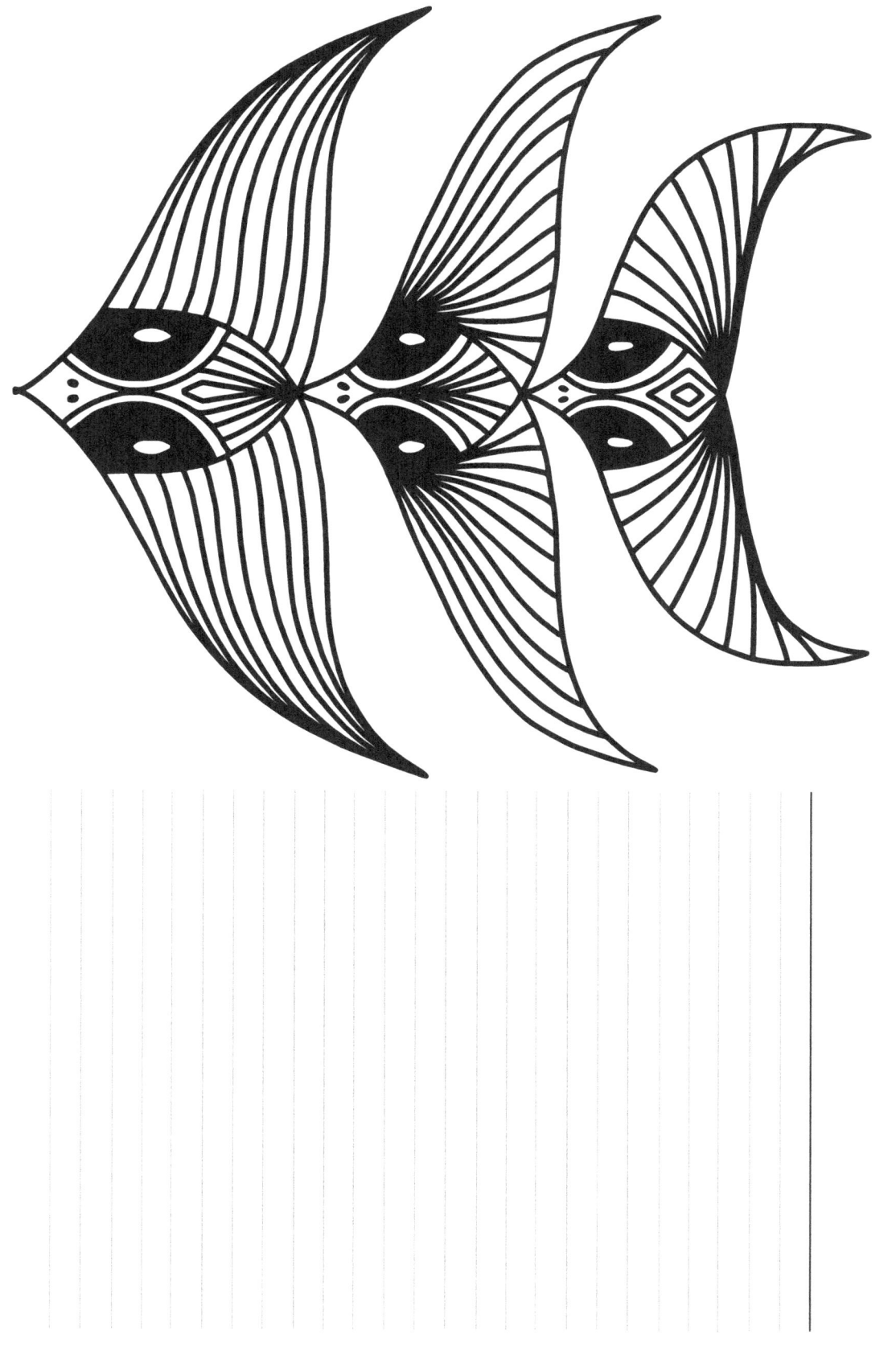

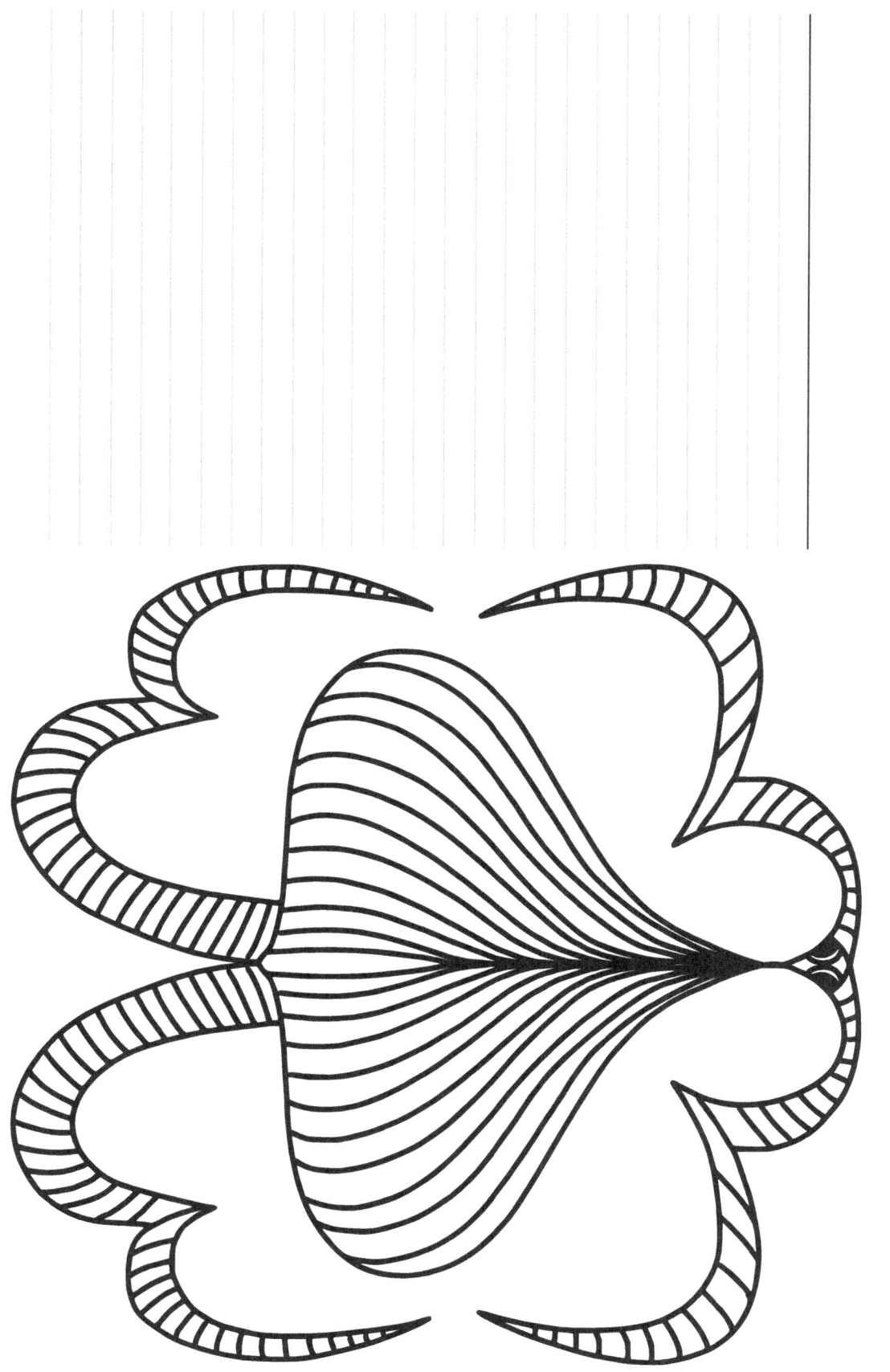

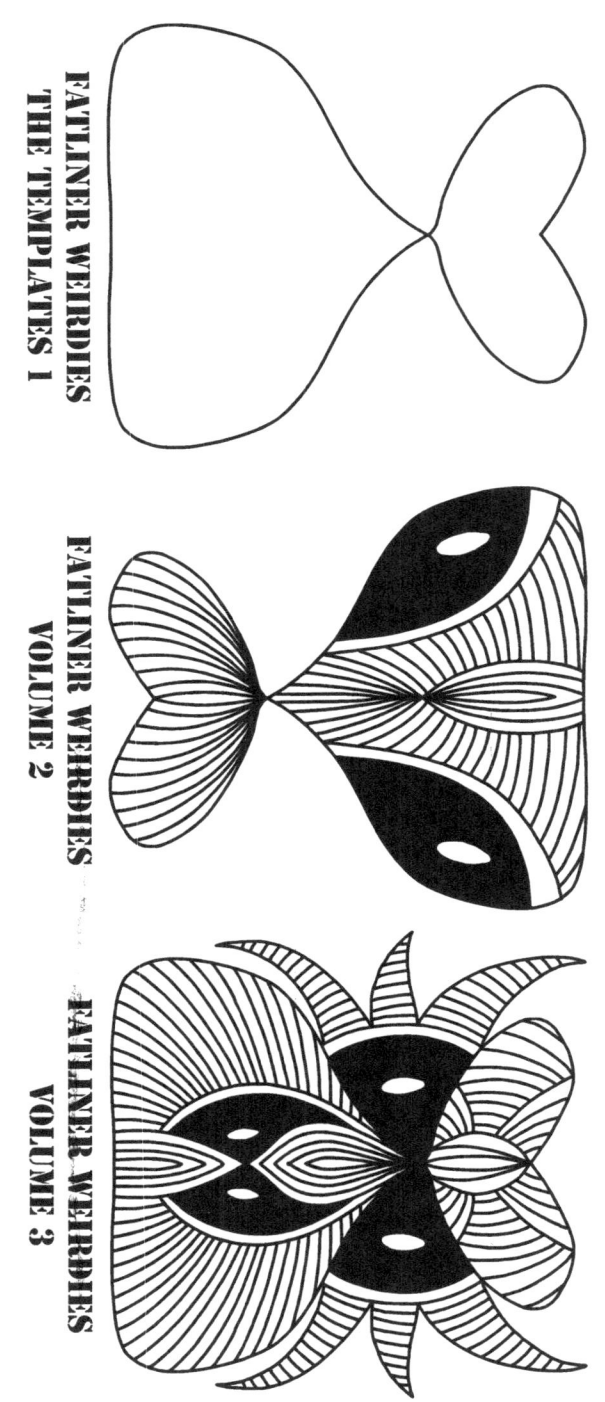

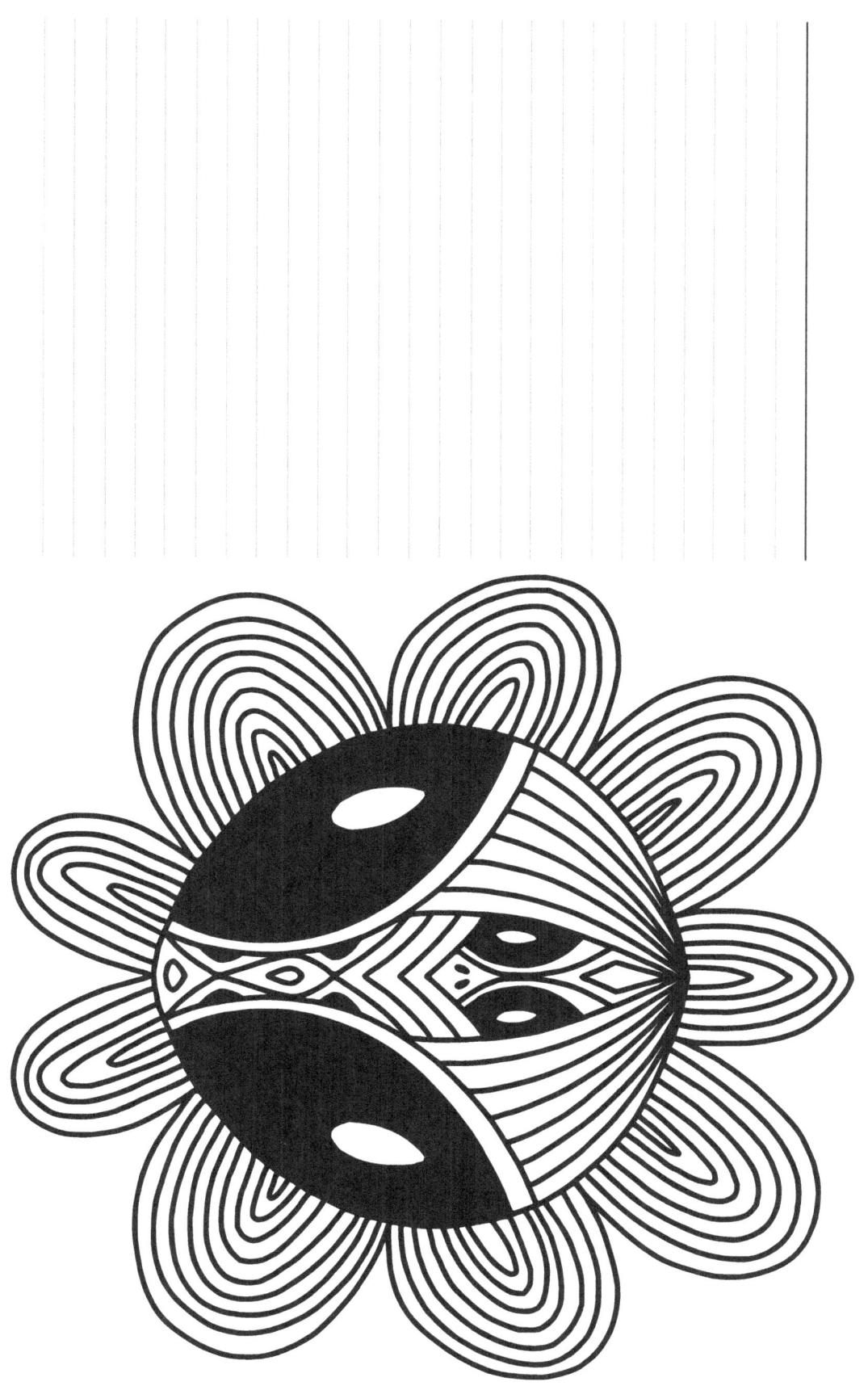

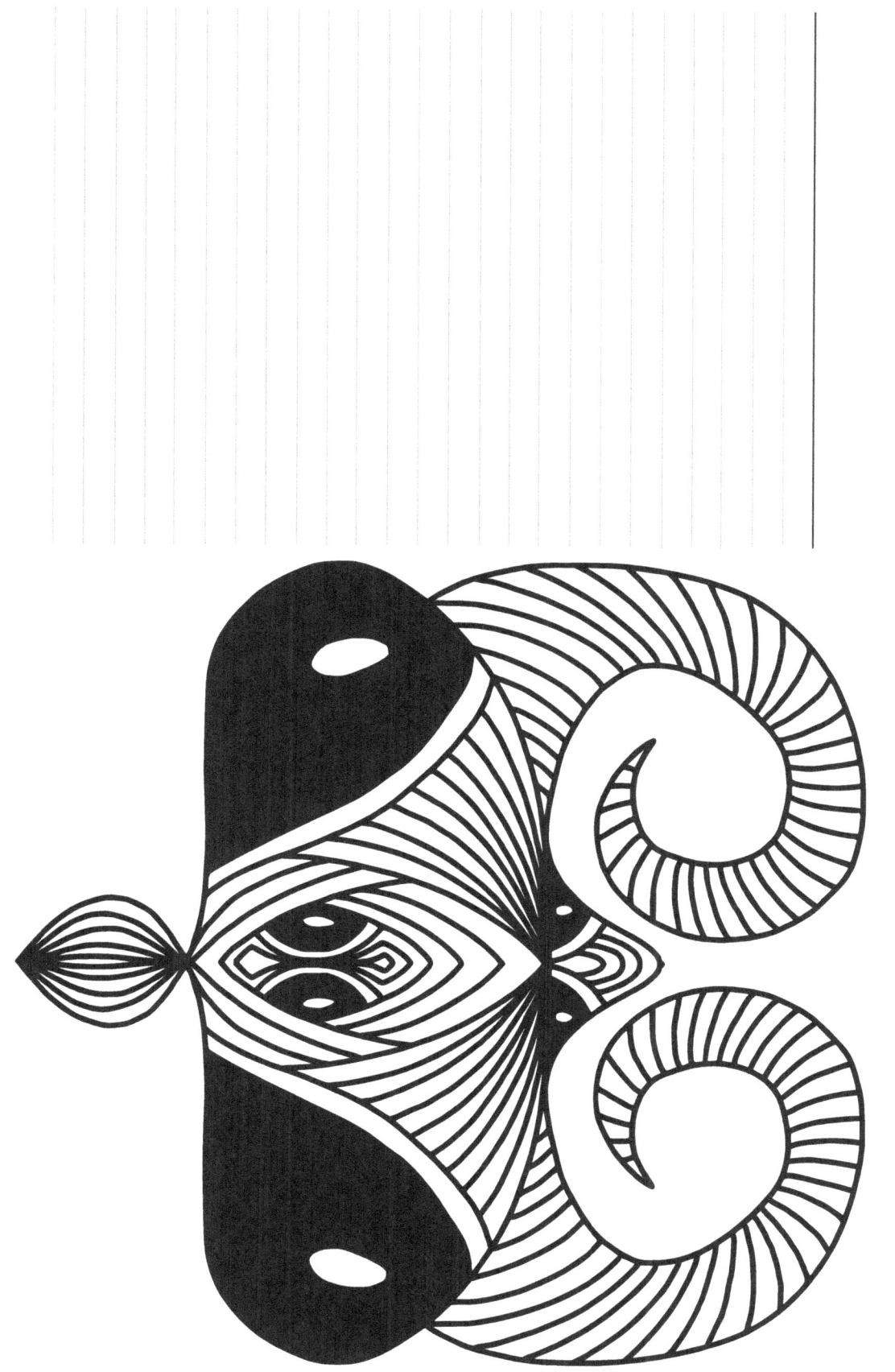

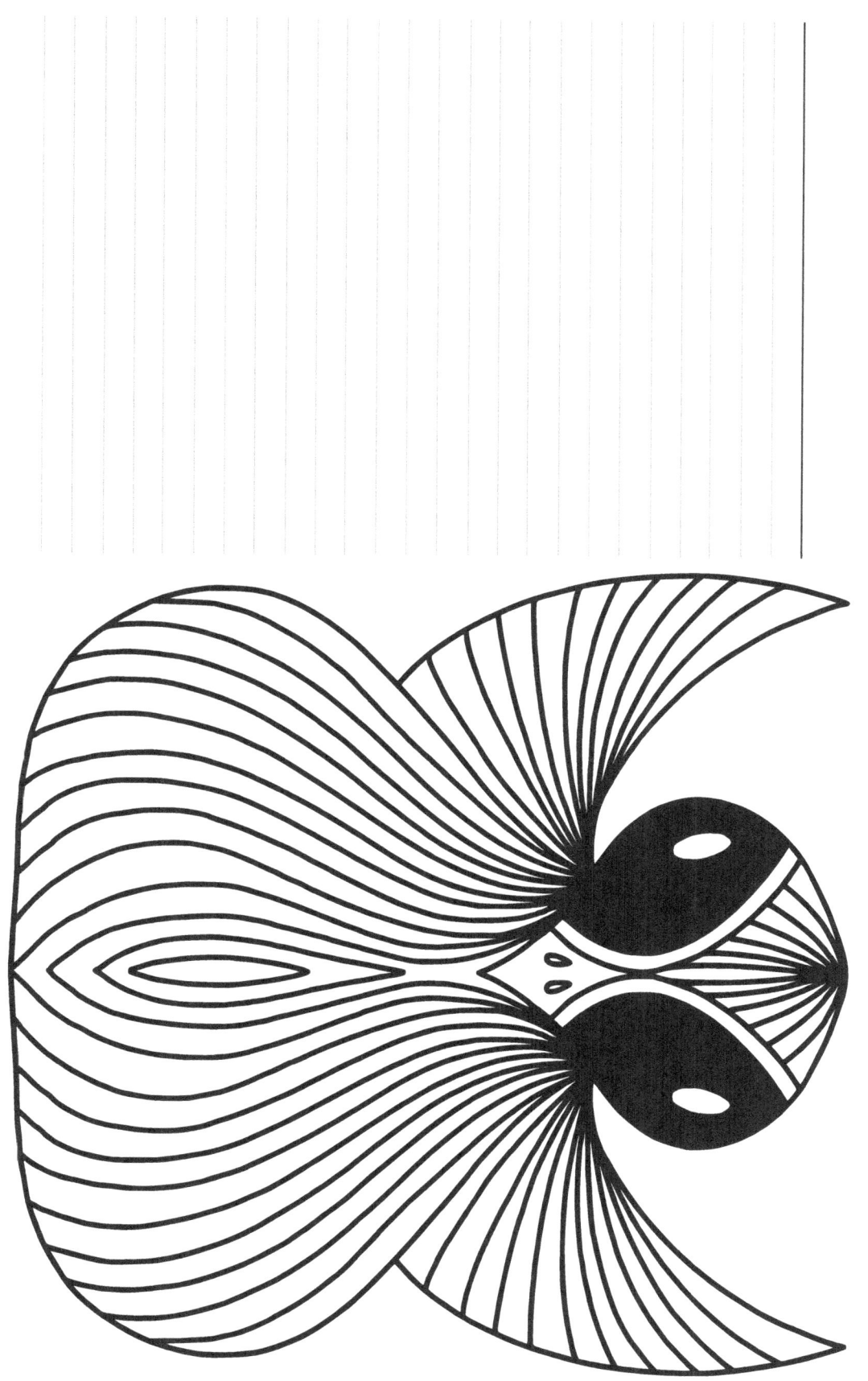

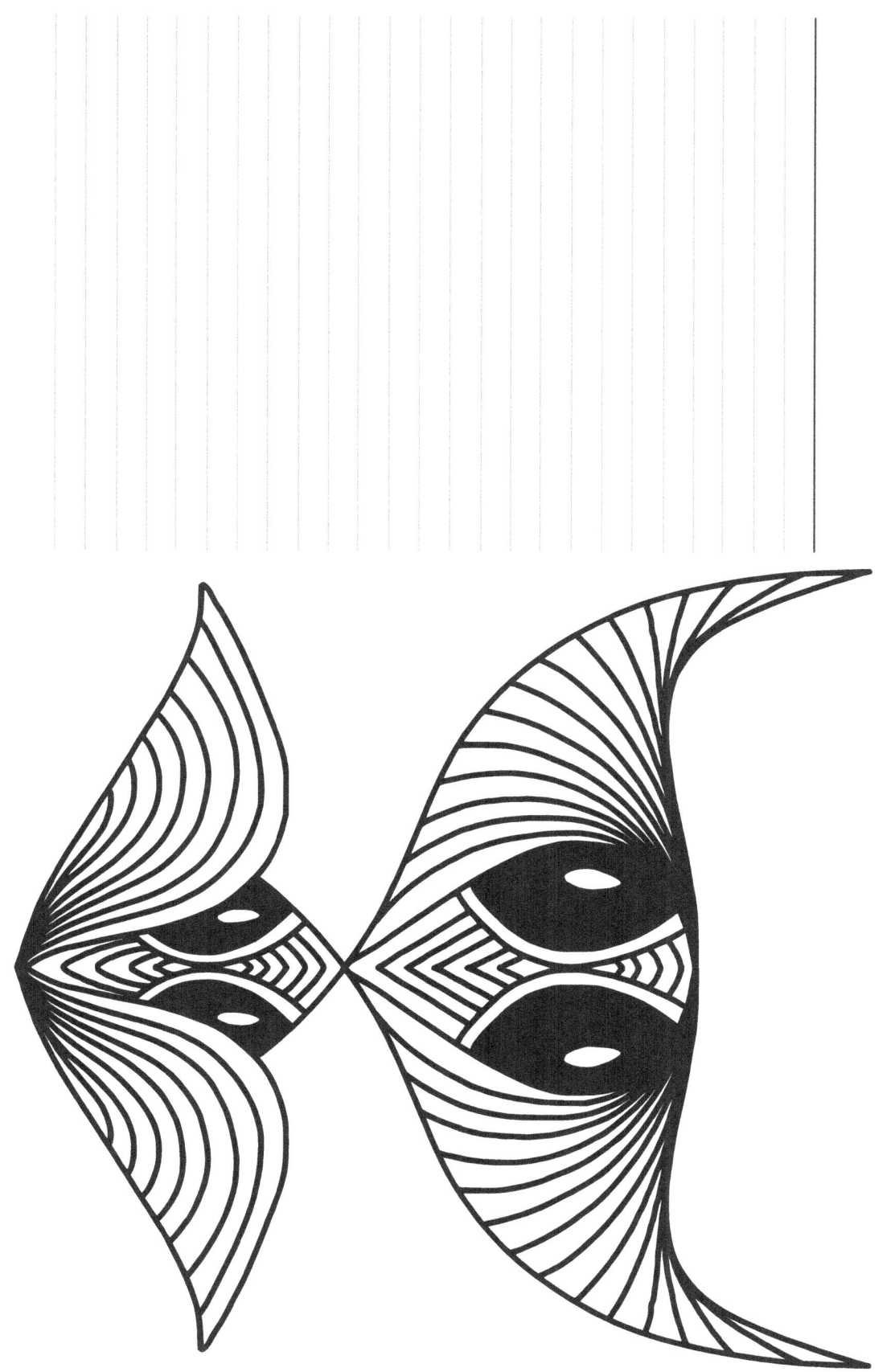

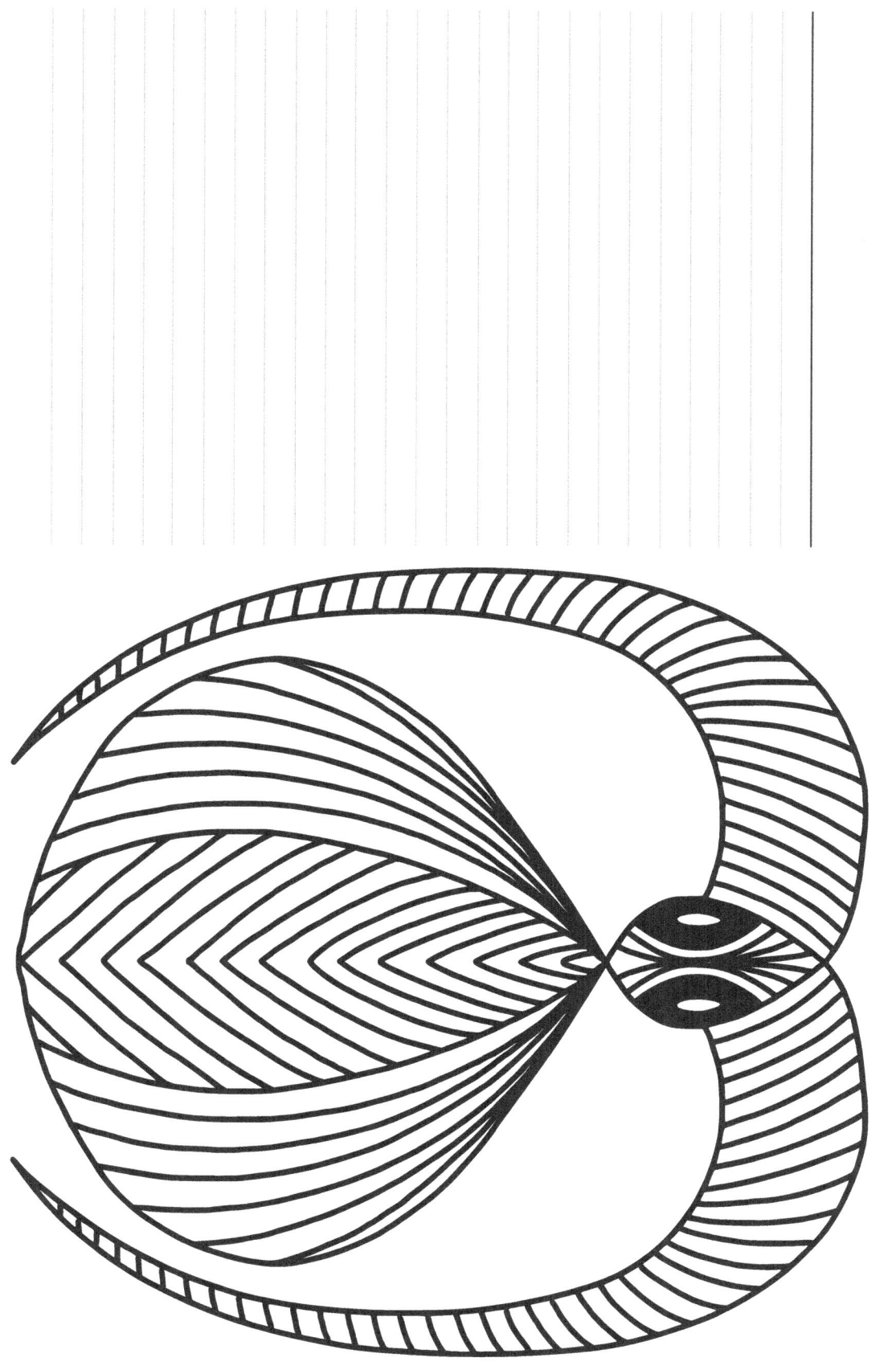

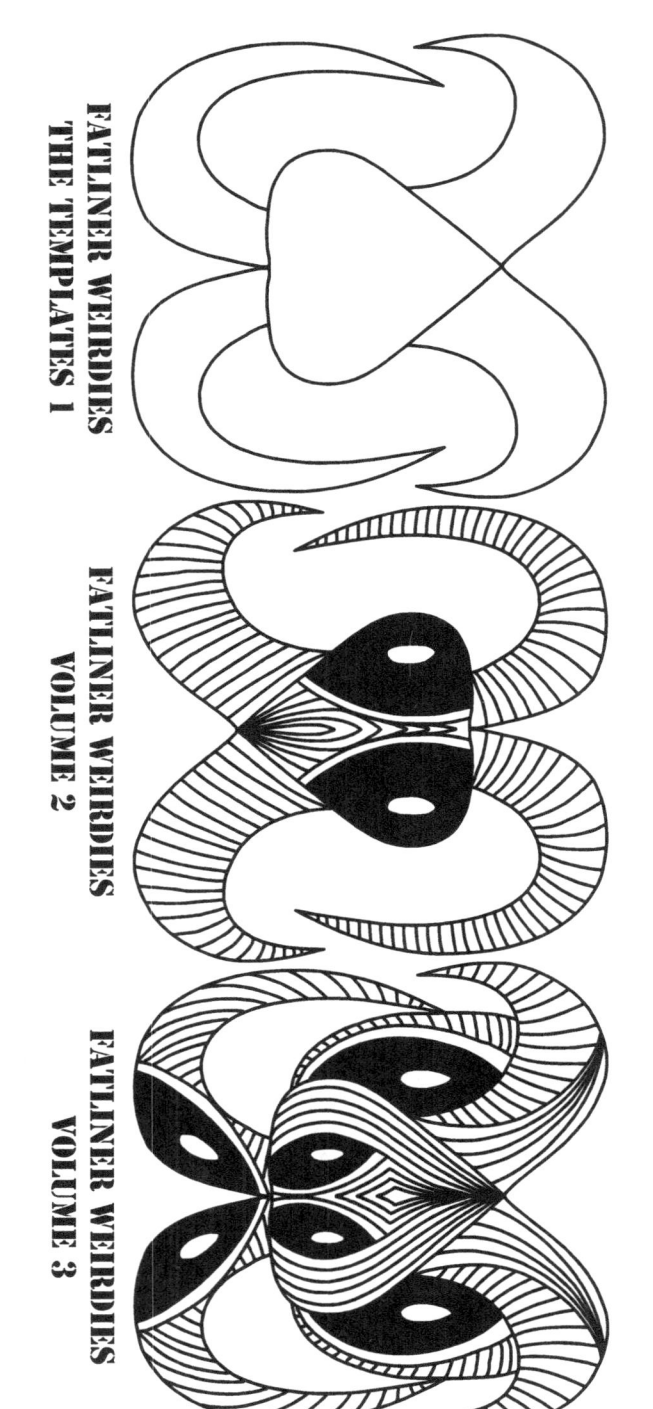

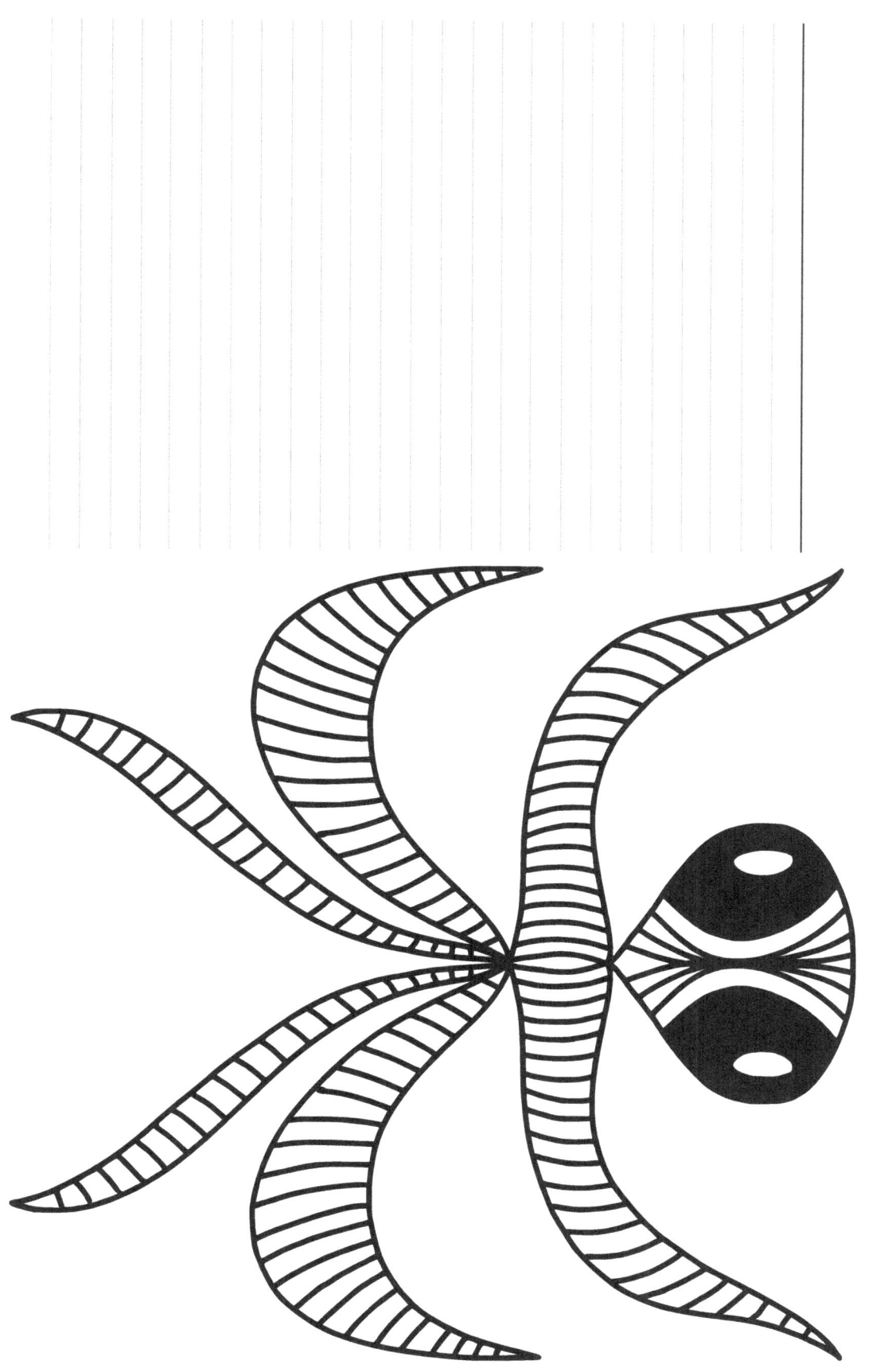

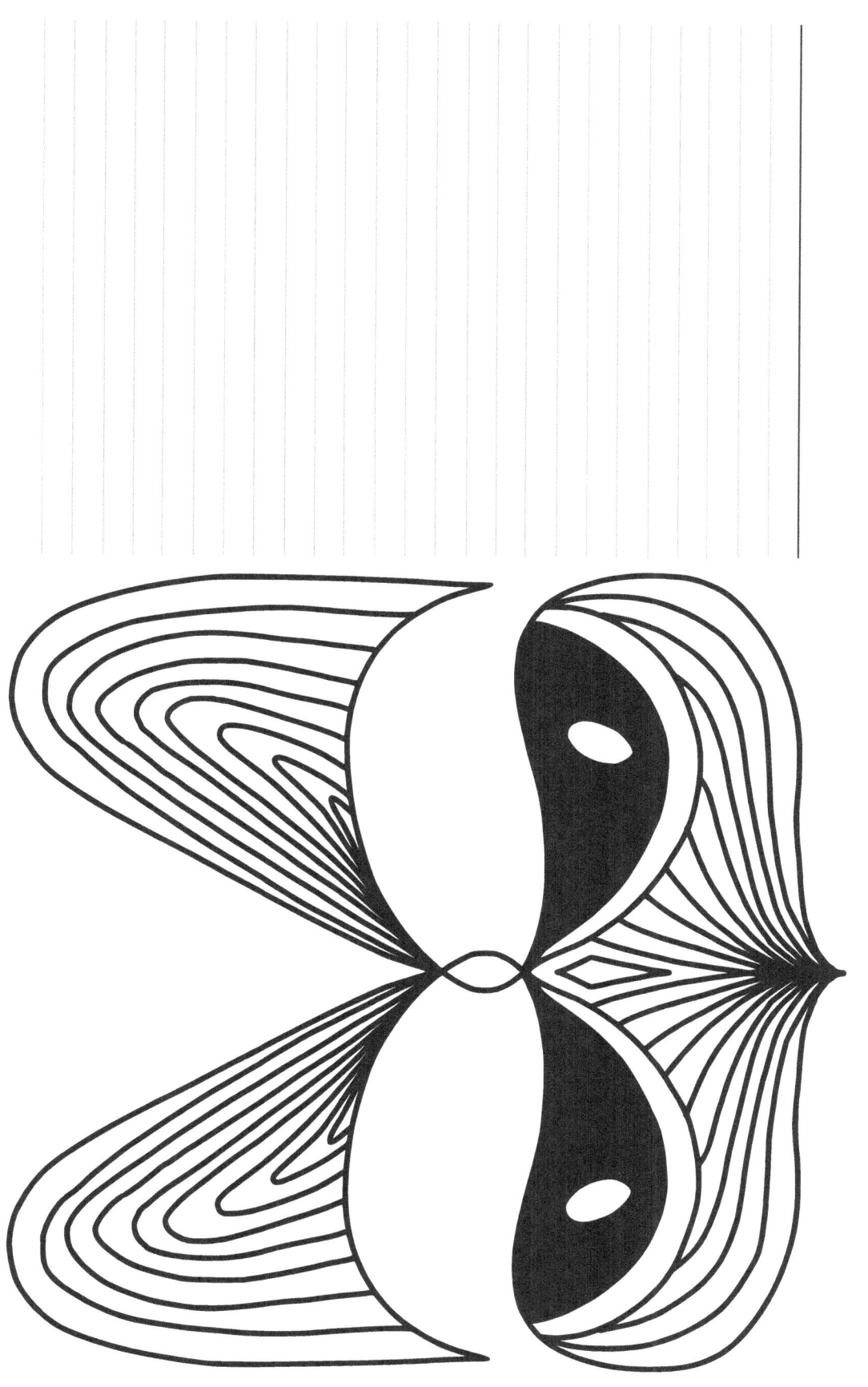

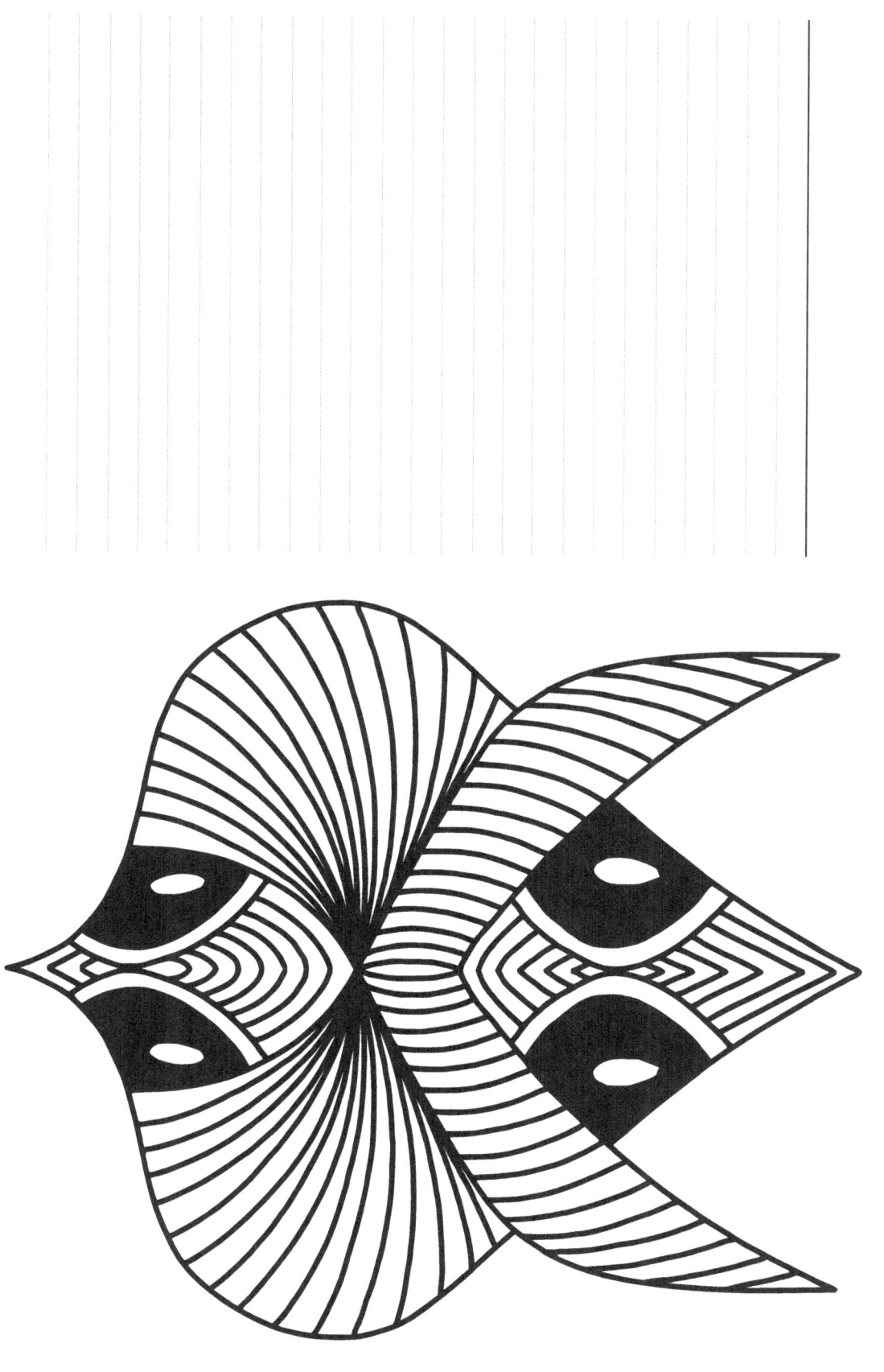

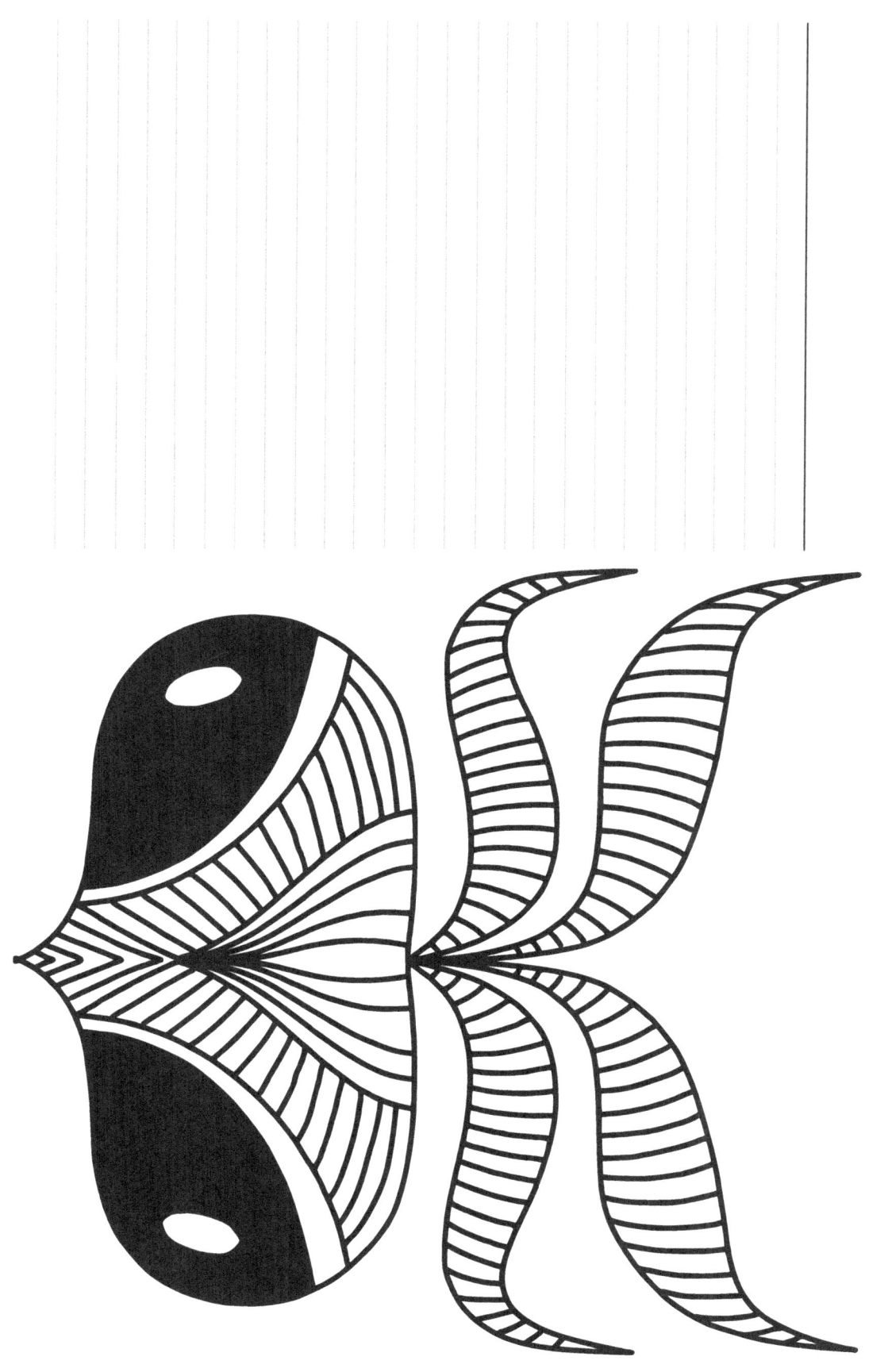

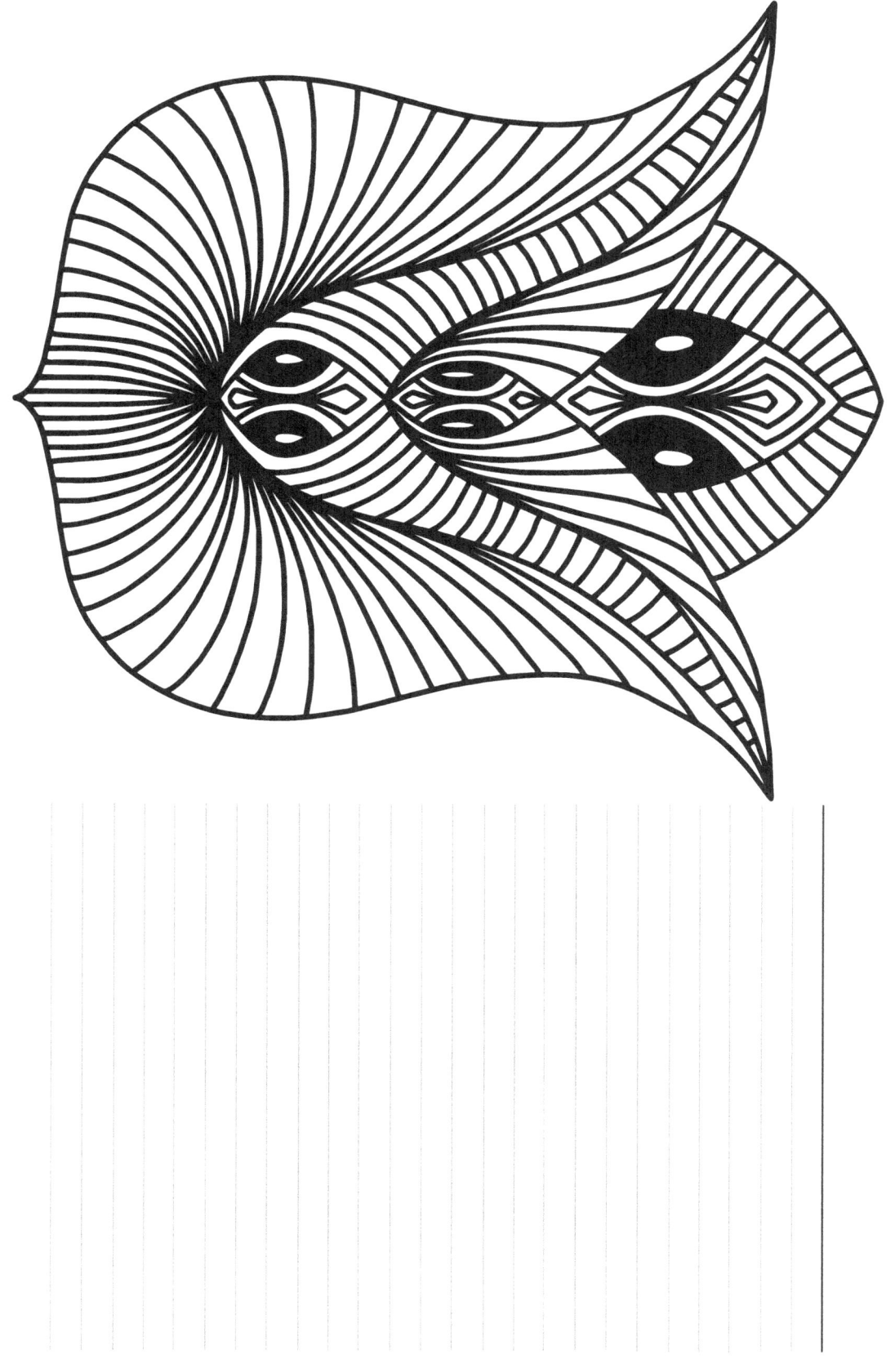

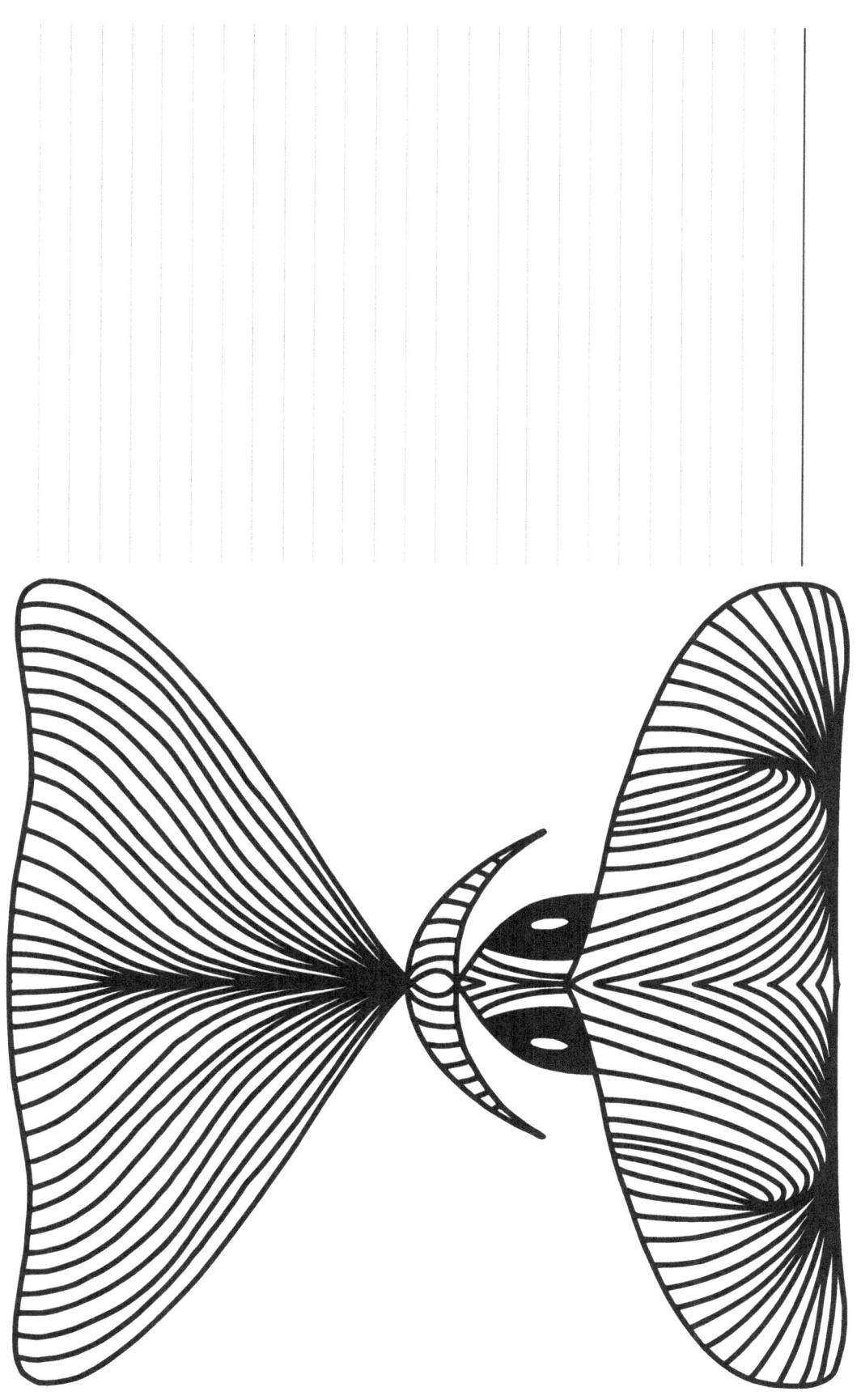

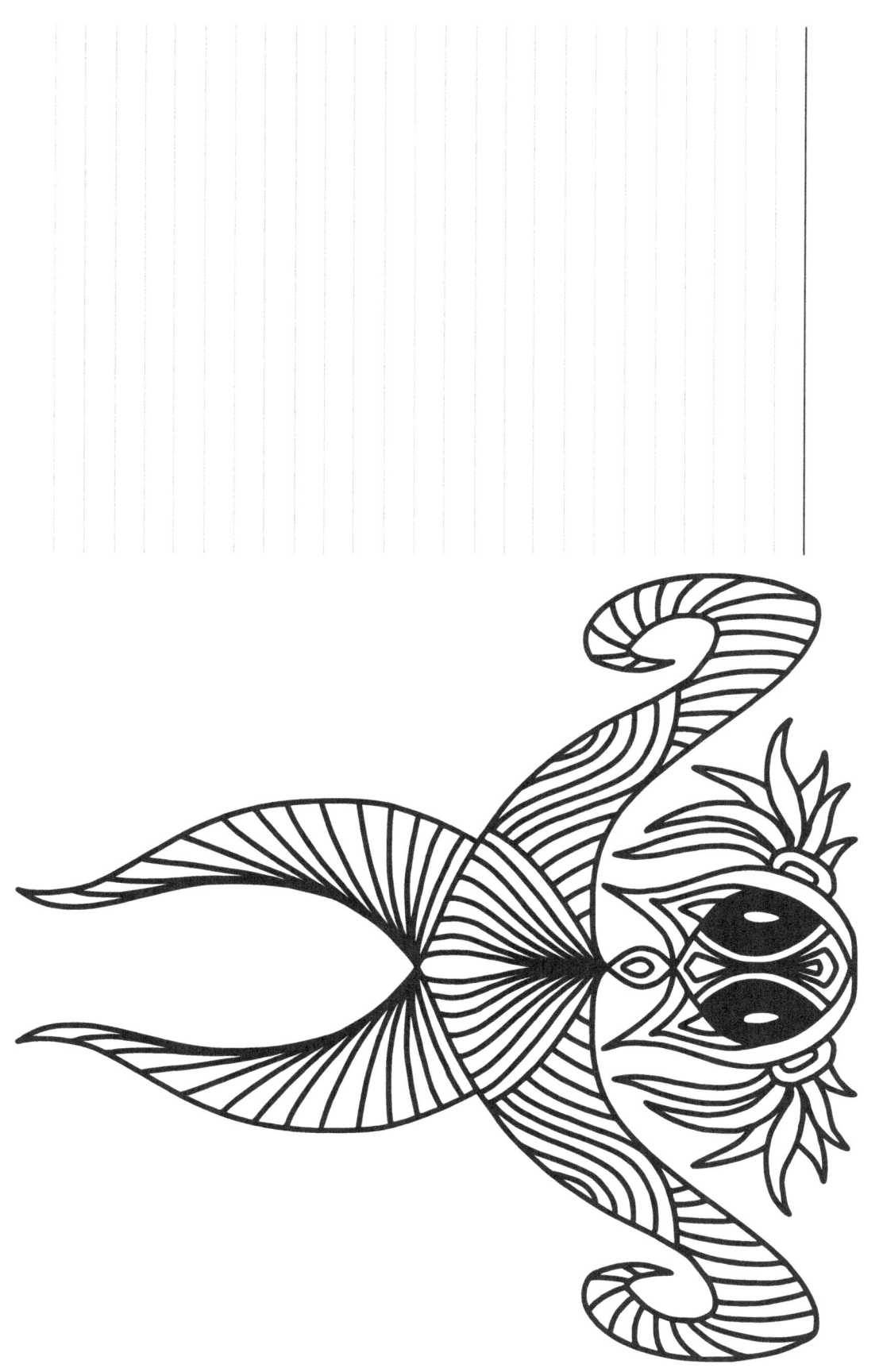

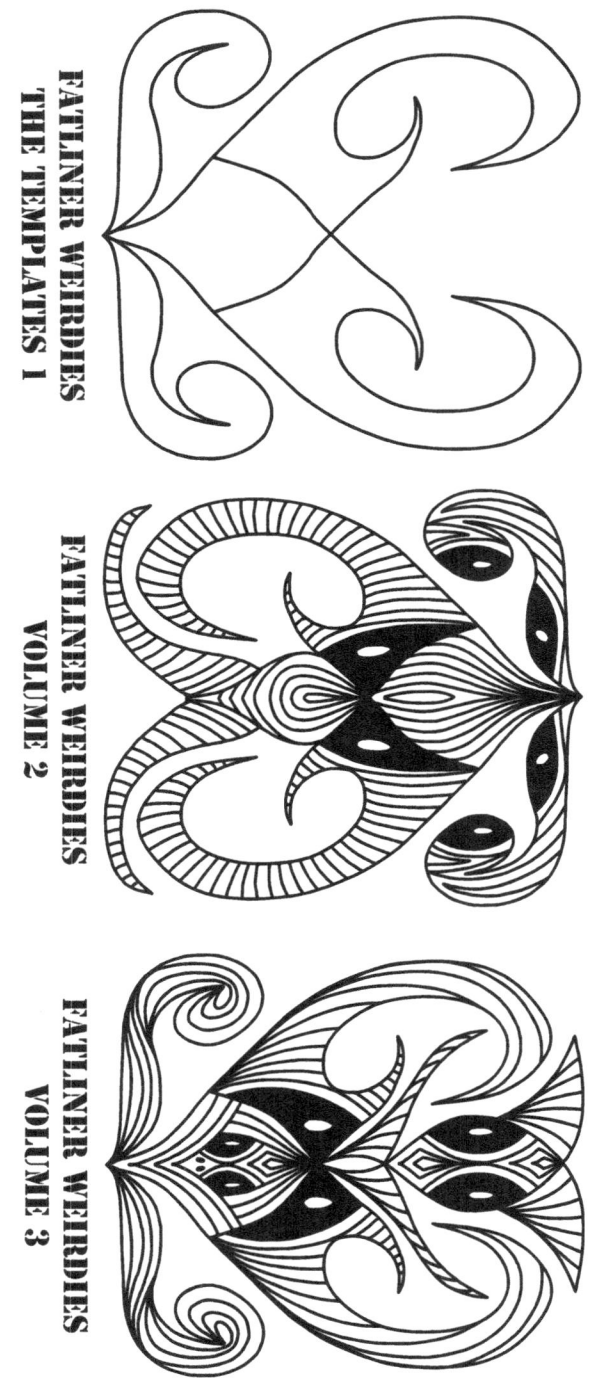

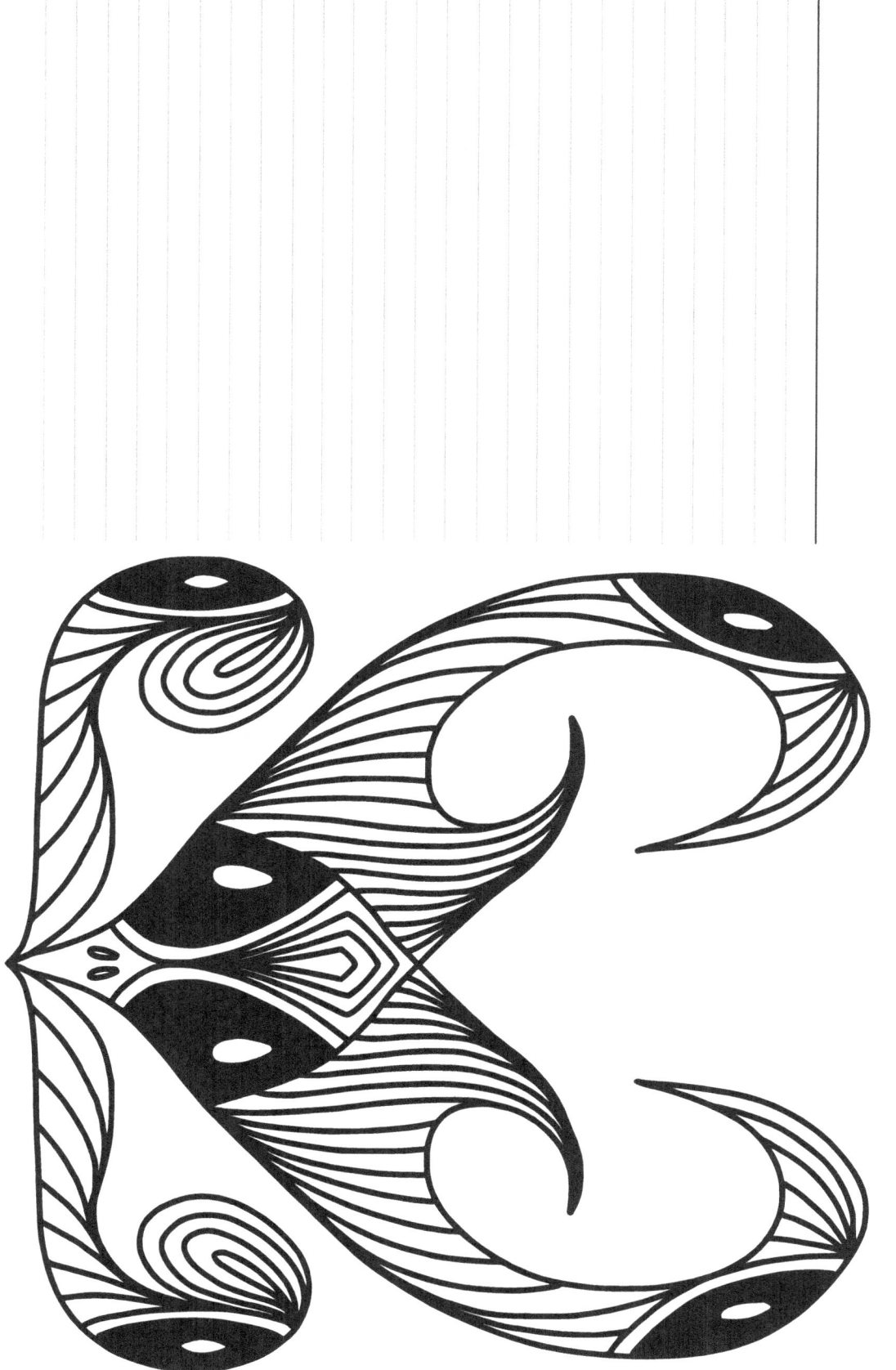

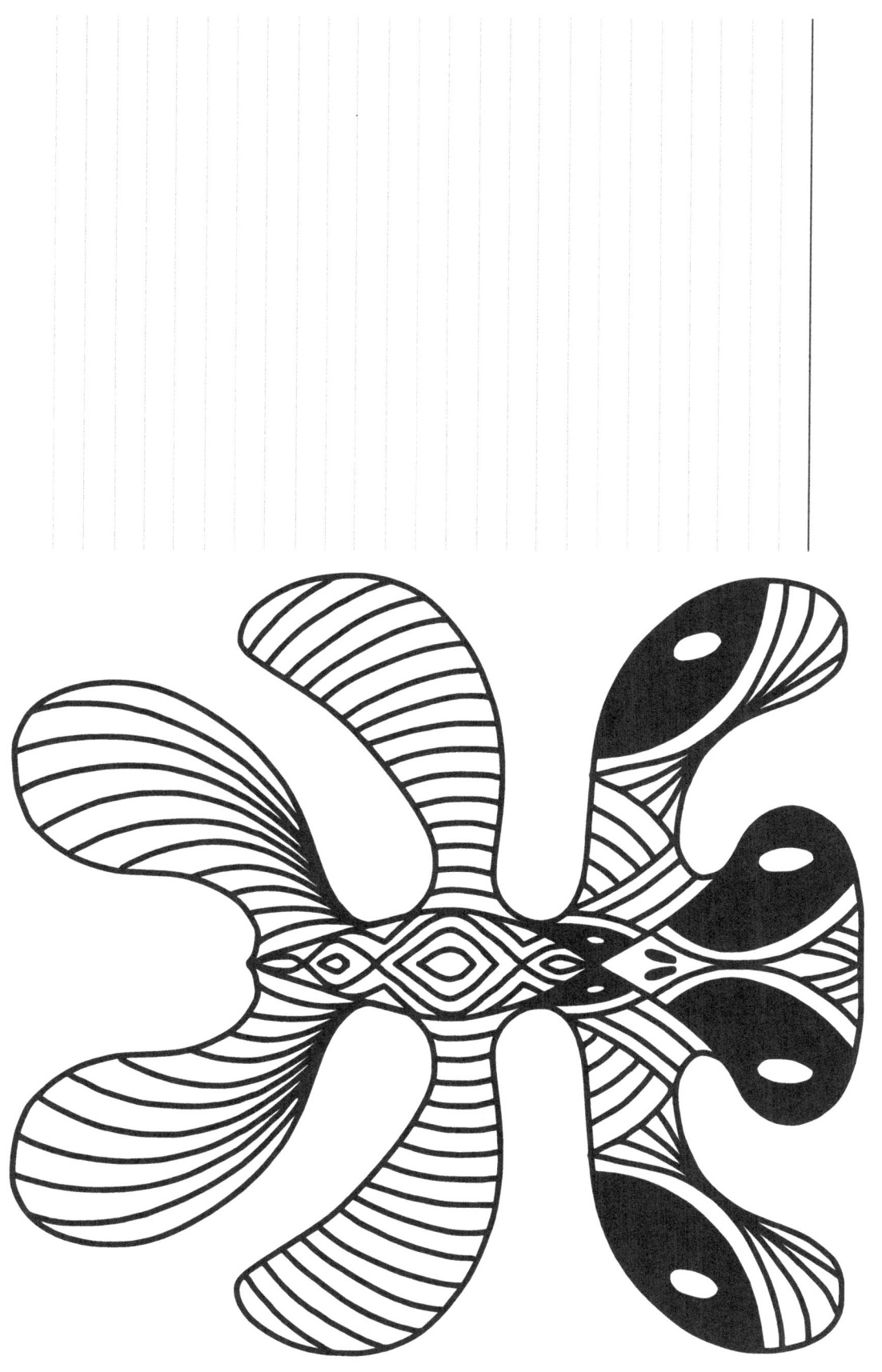

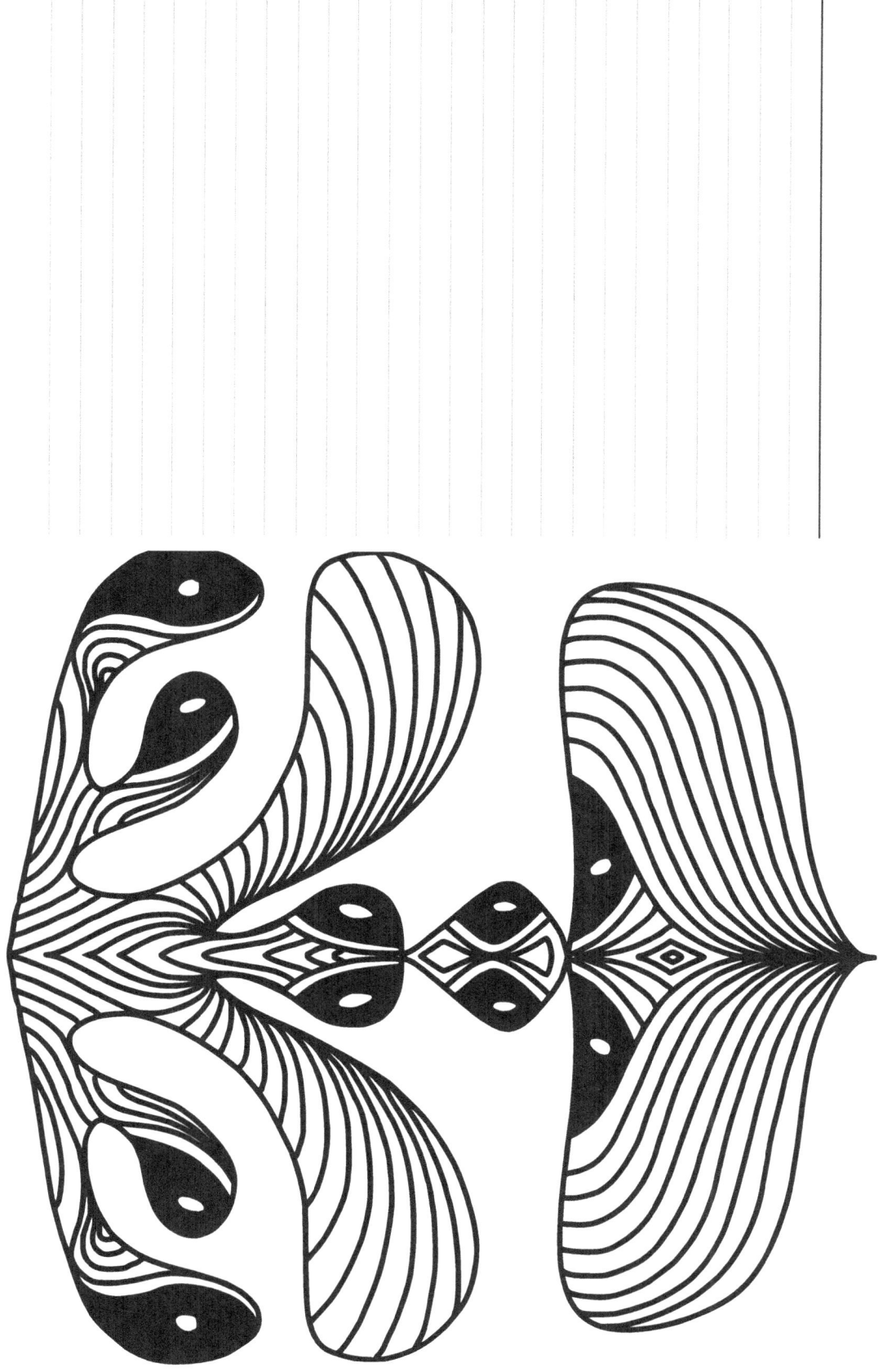

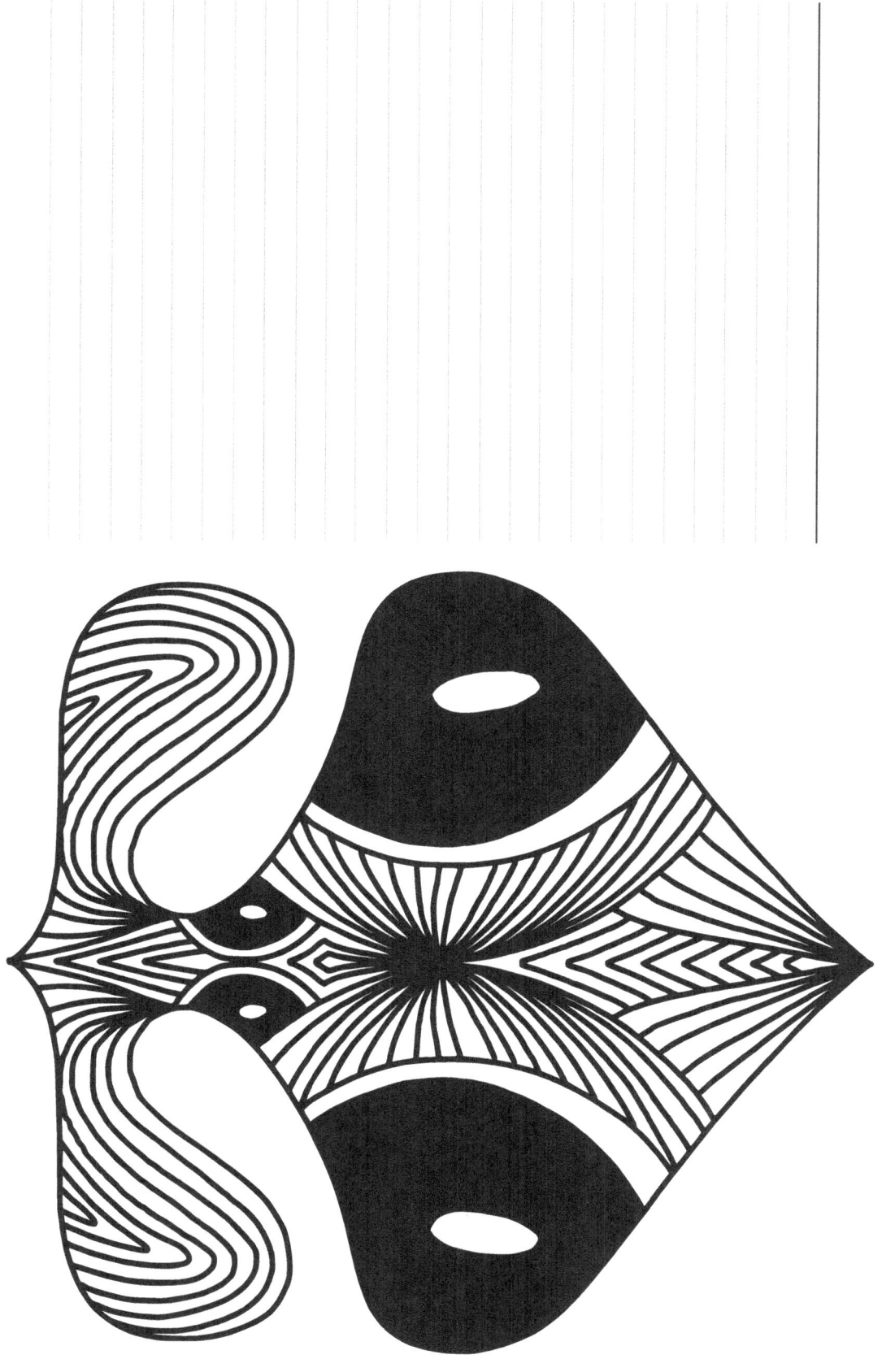

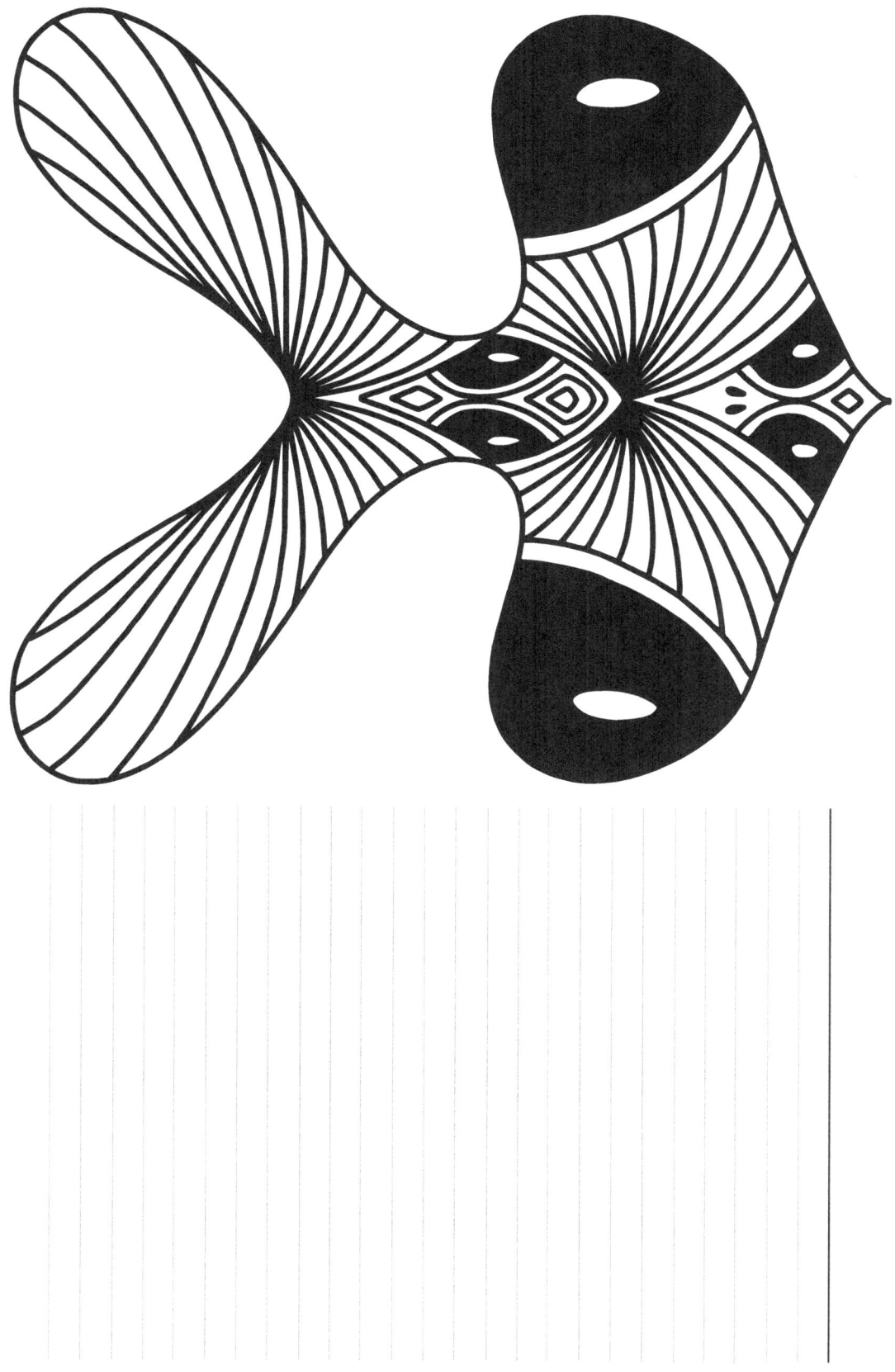

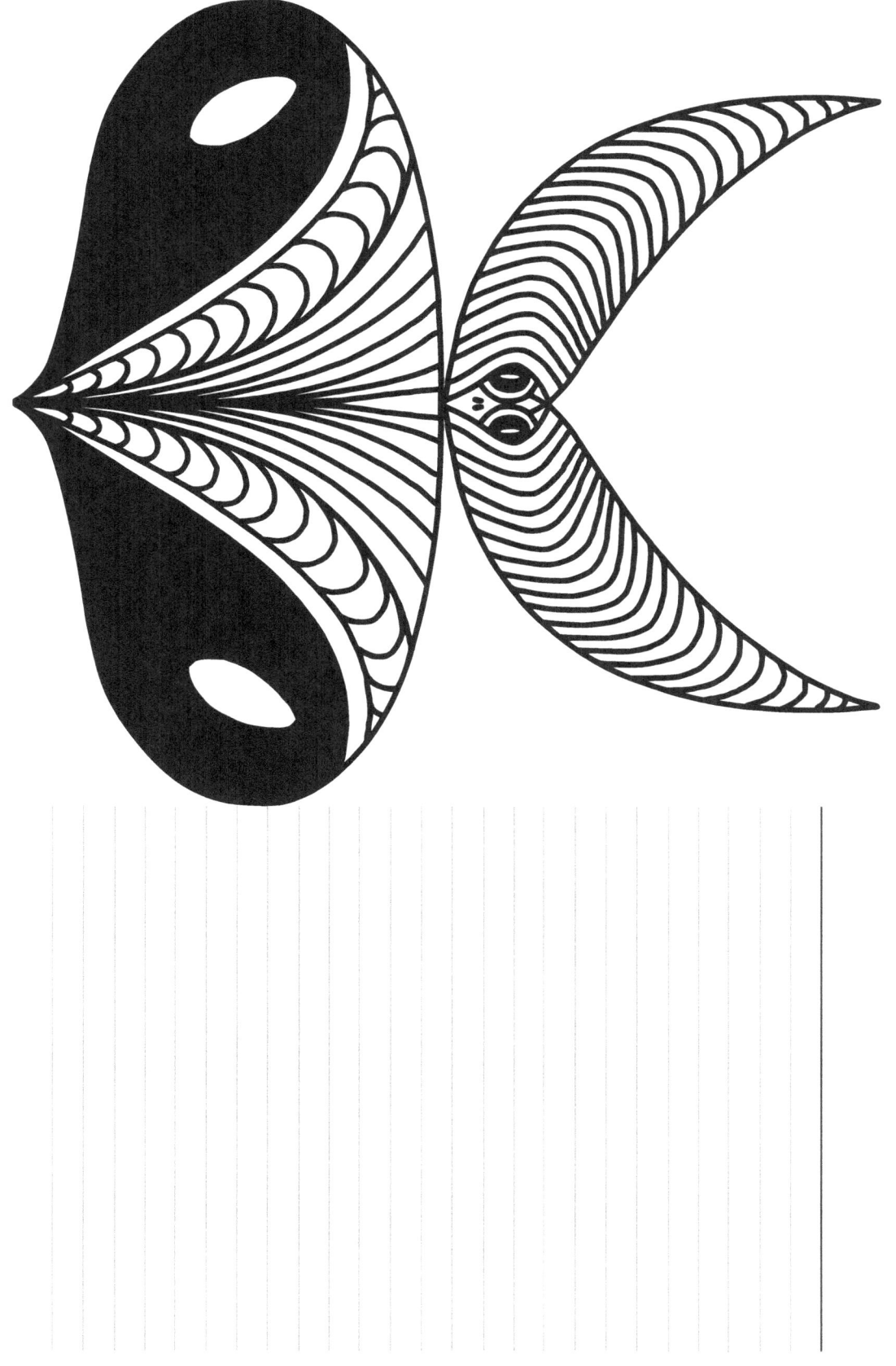

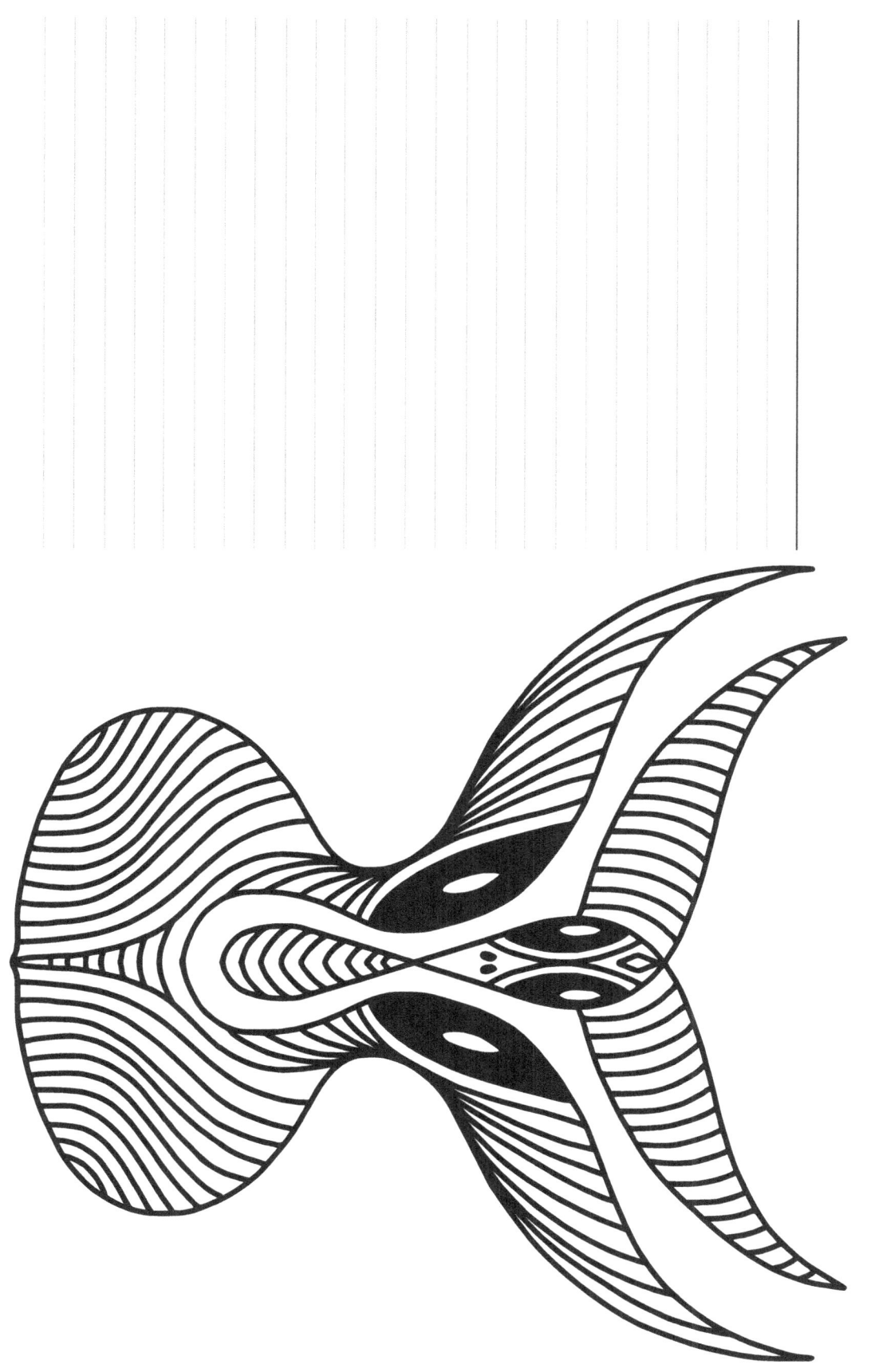

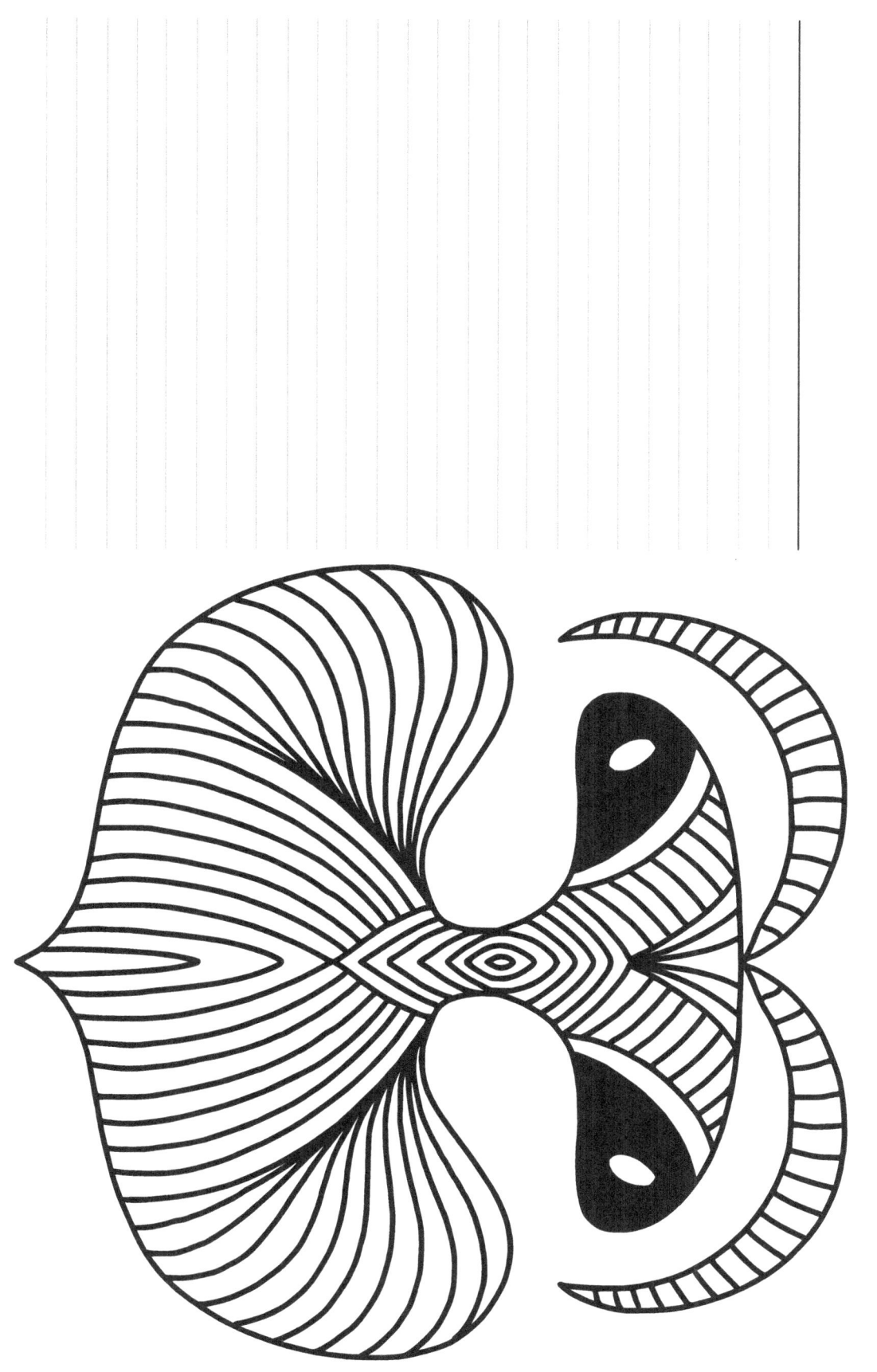

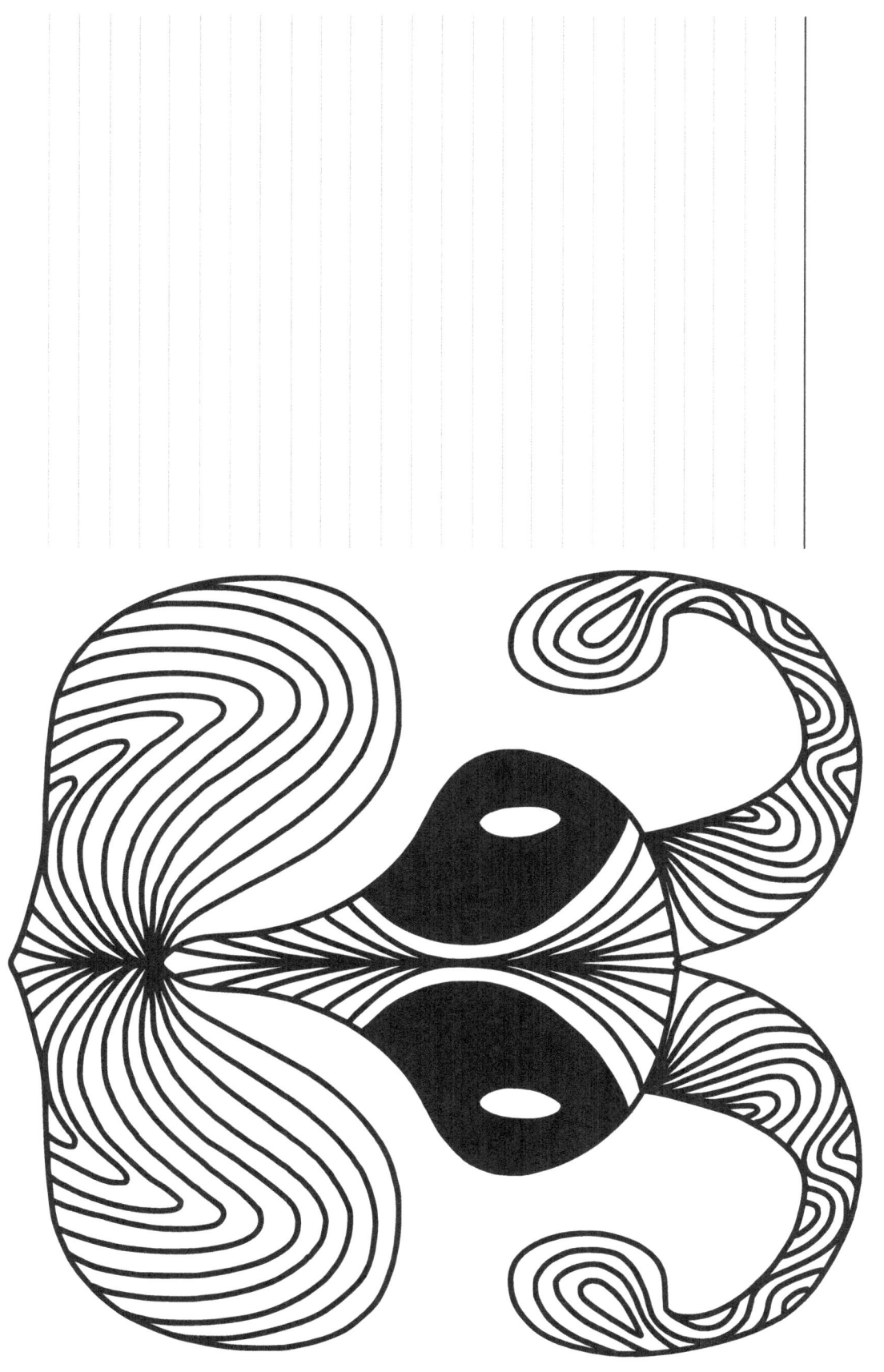

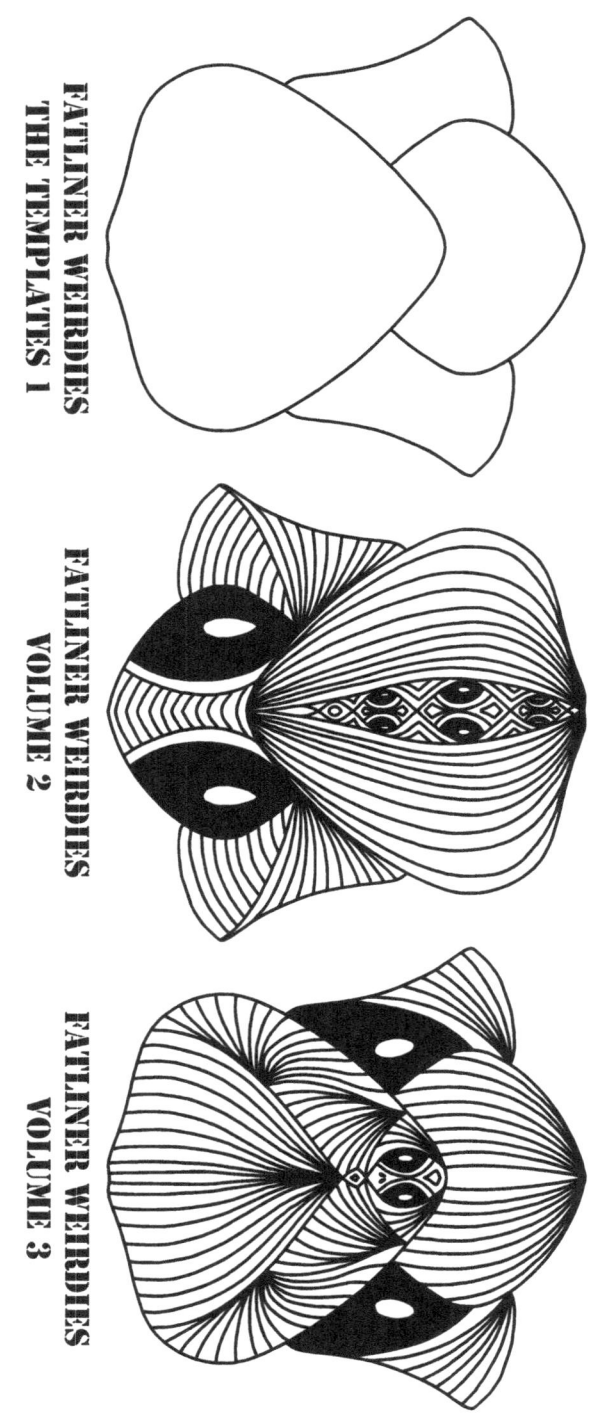

FATLINER WEIRDIES
THE TEMPLATES 1

FATLINER WEIRDIES
VOLUME 2

FATLINER WEIRDIES
VOLUME 3

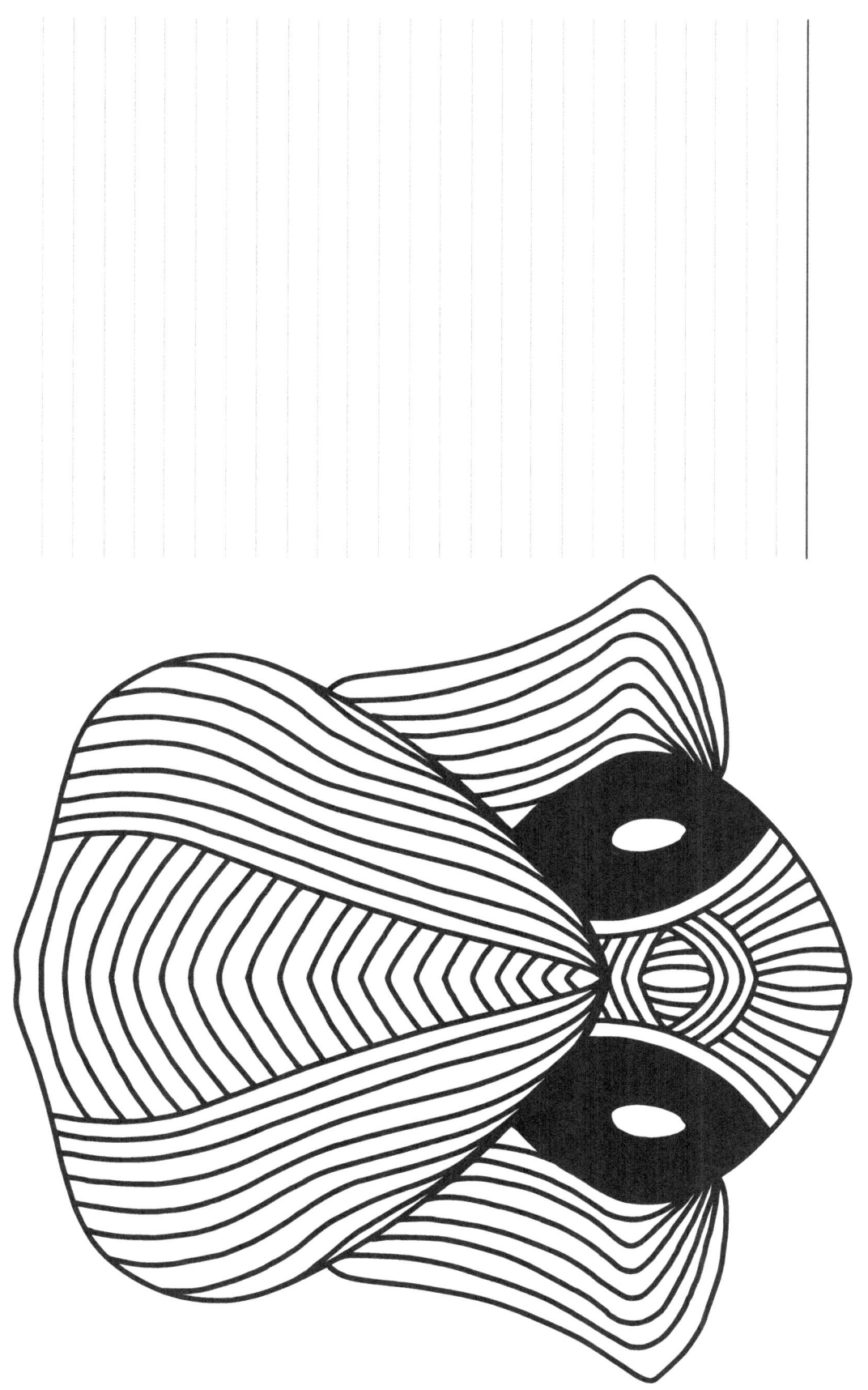

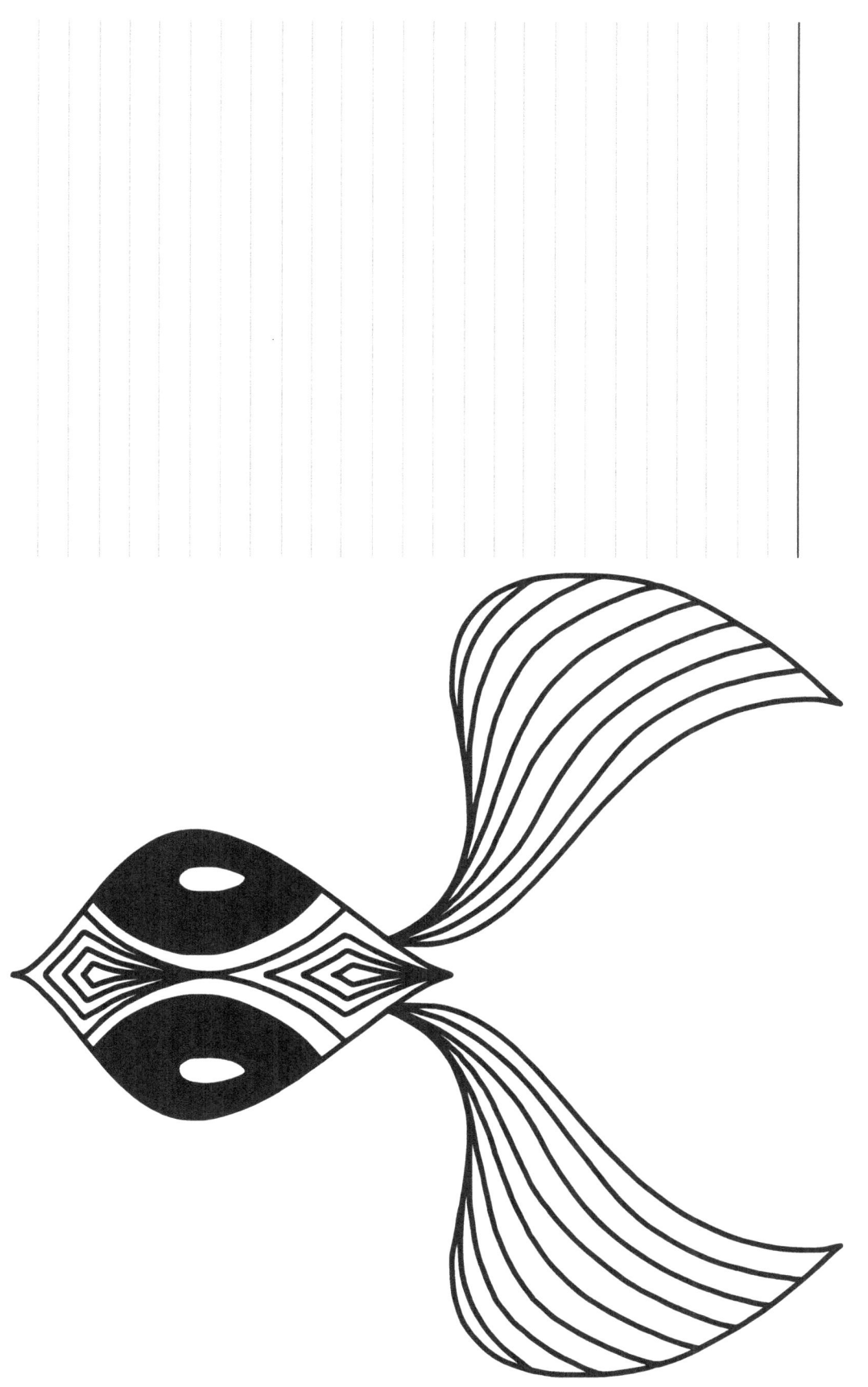

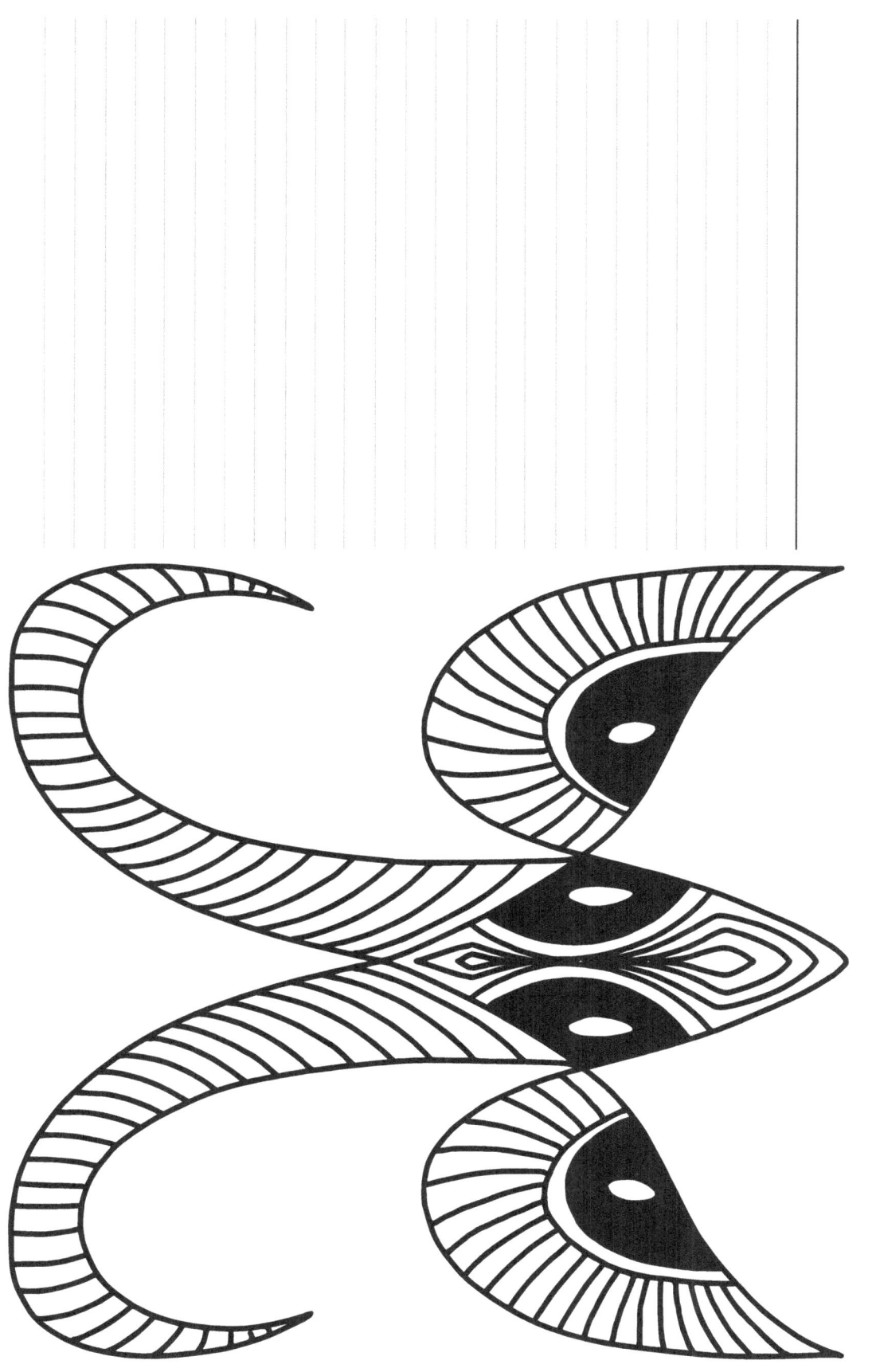

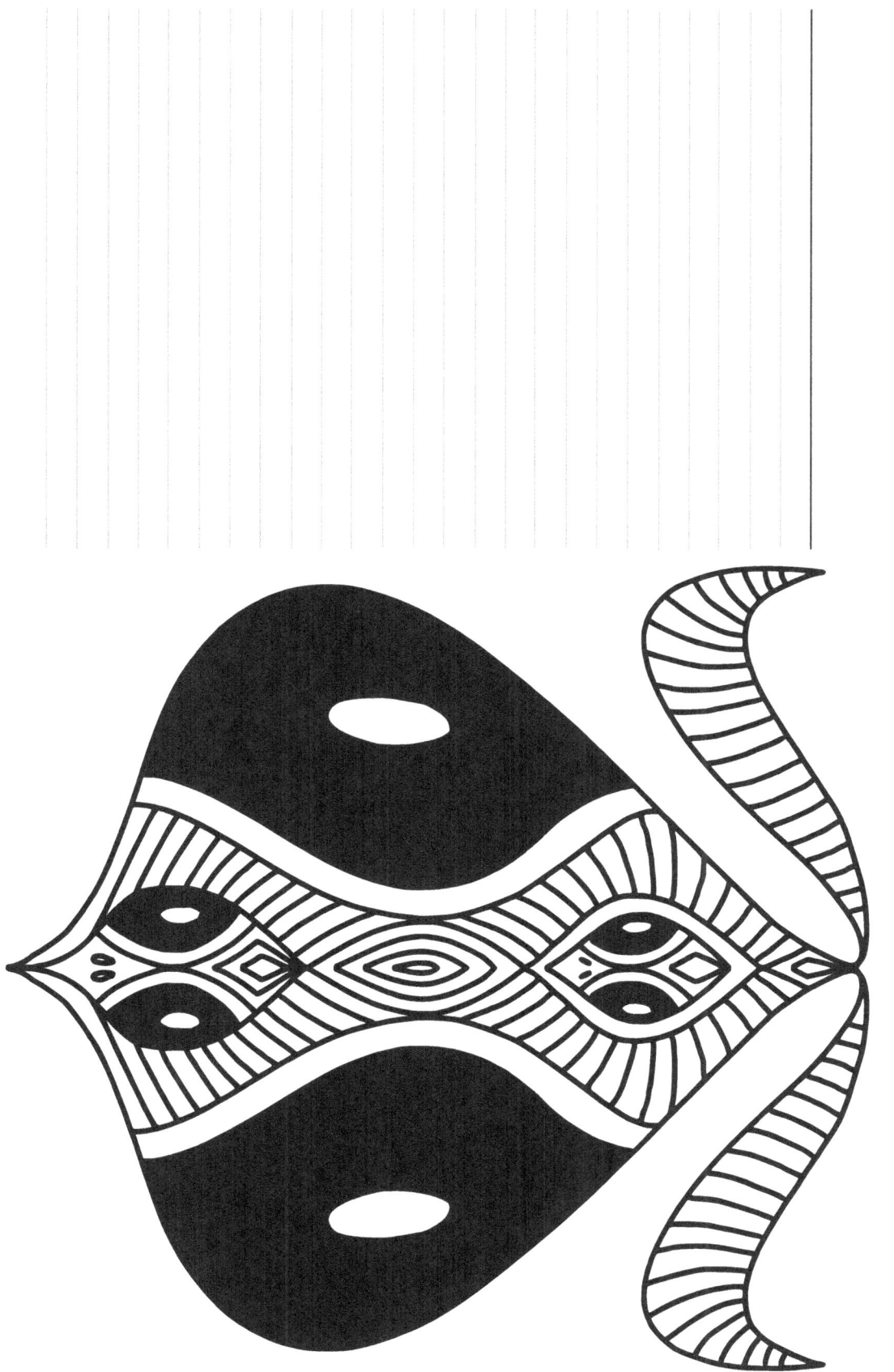

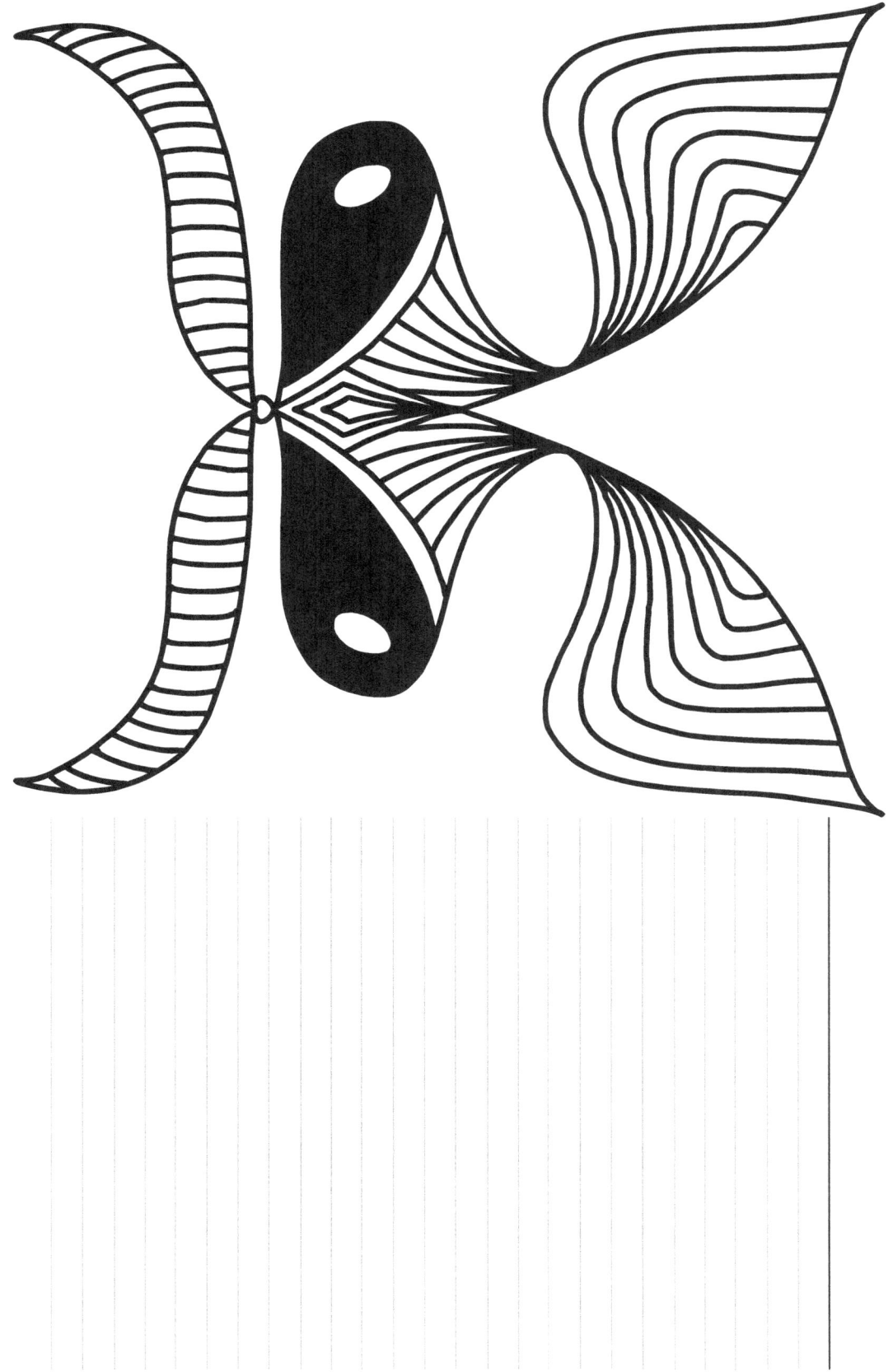

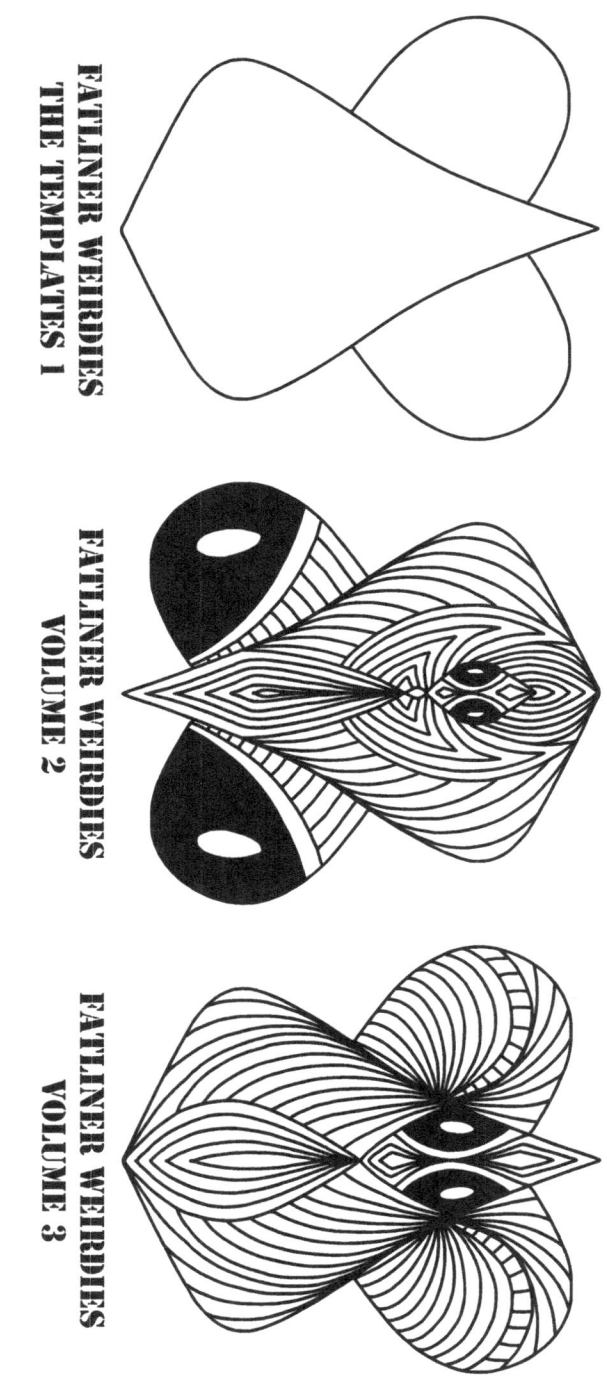

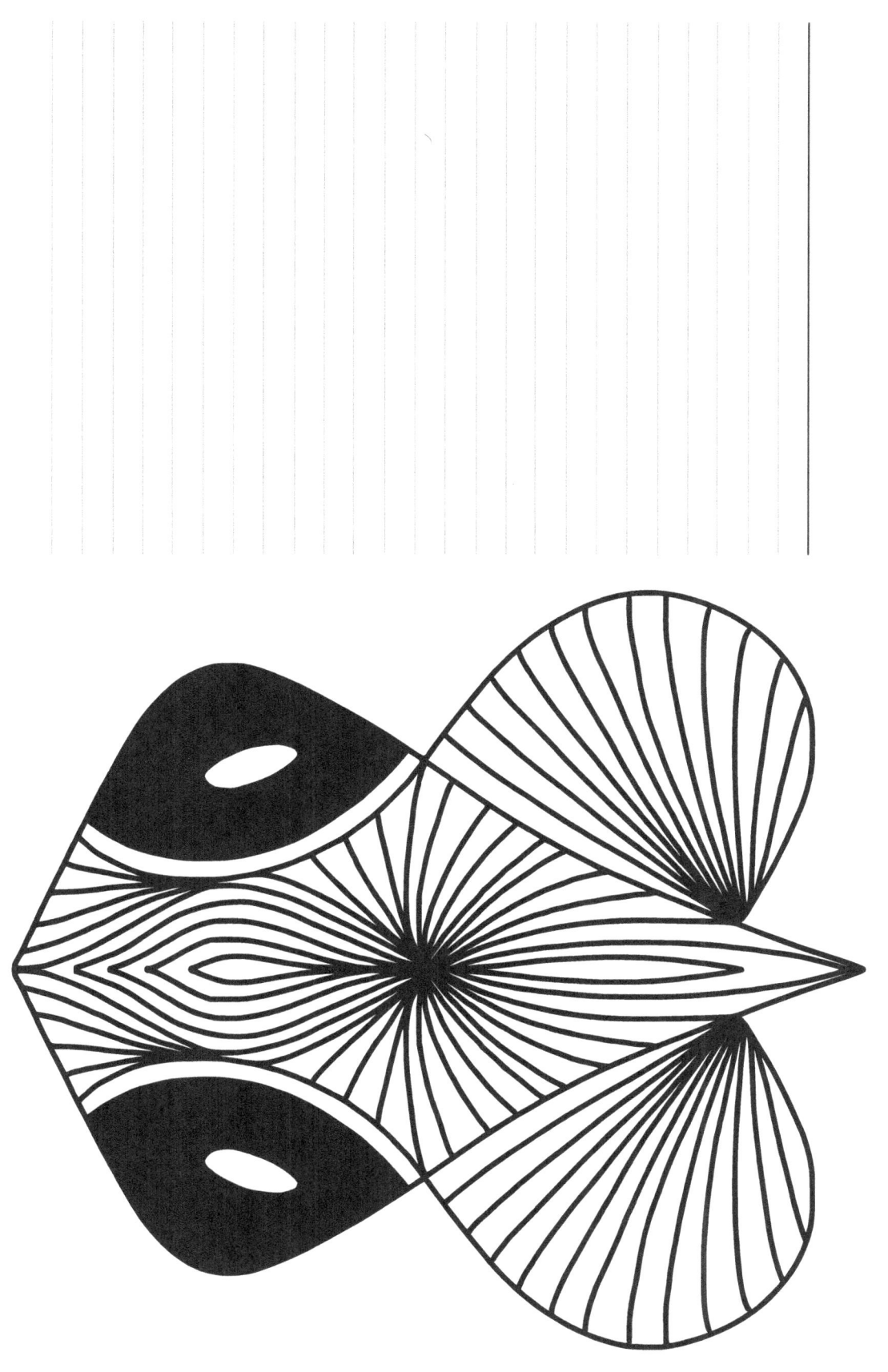

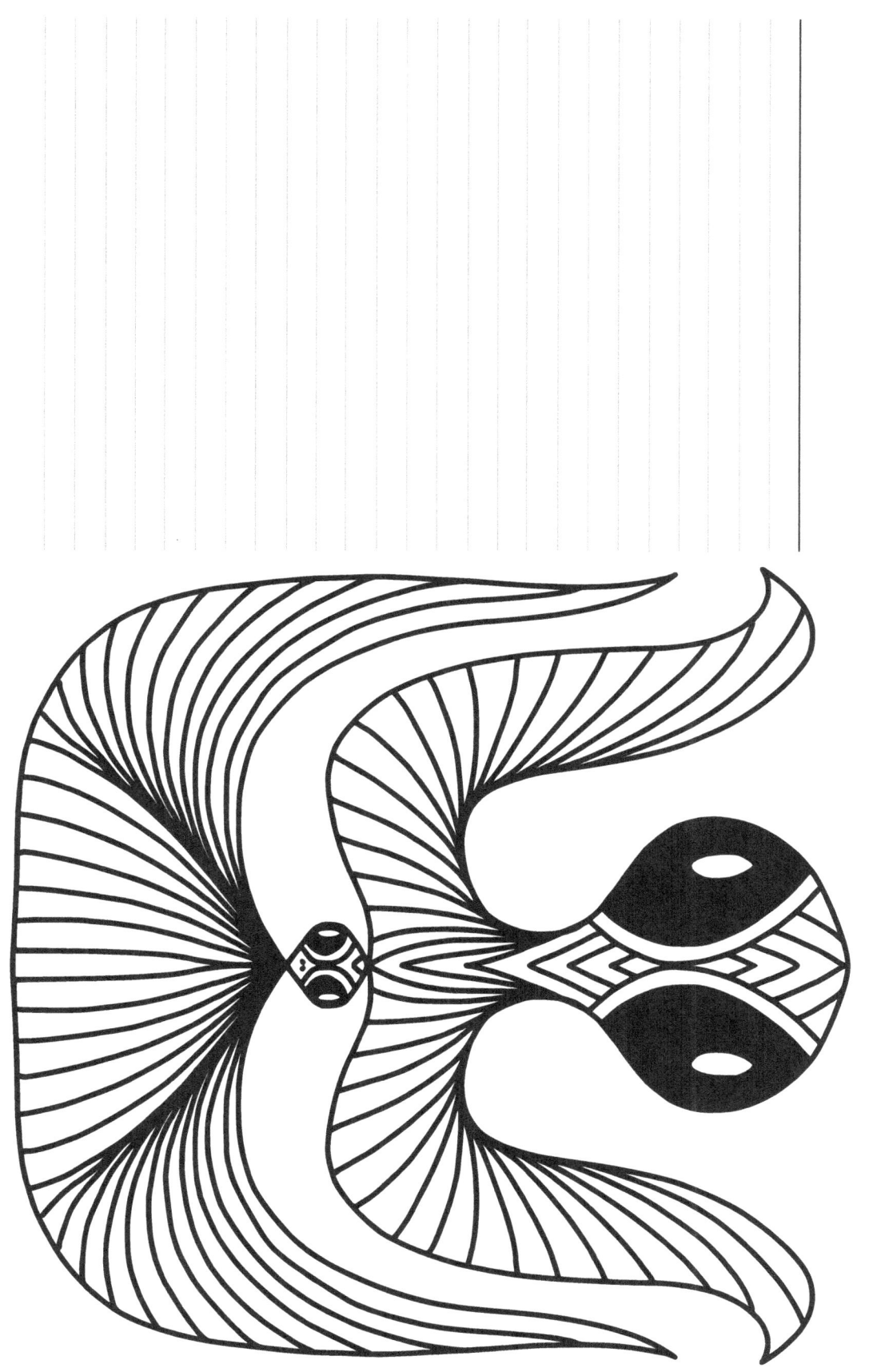

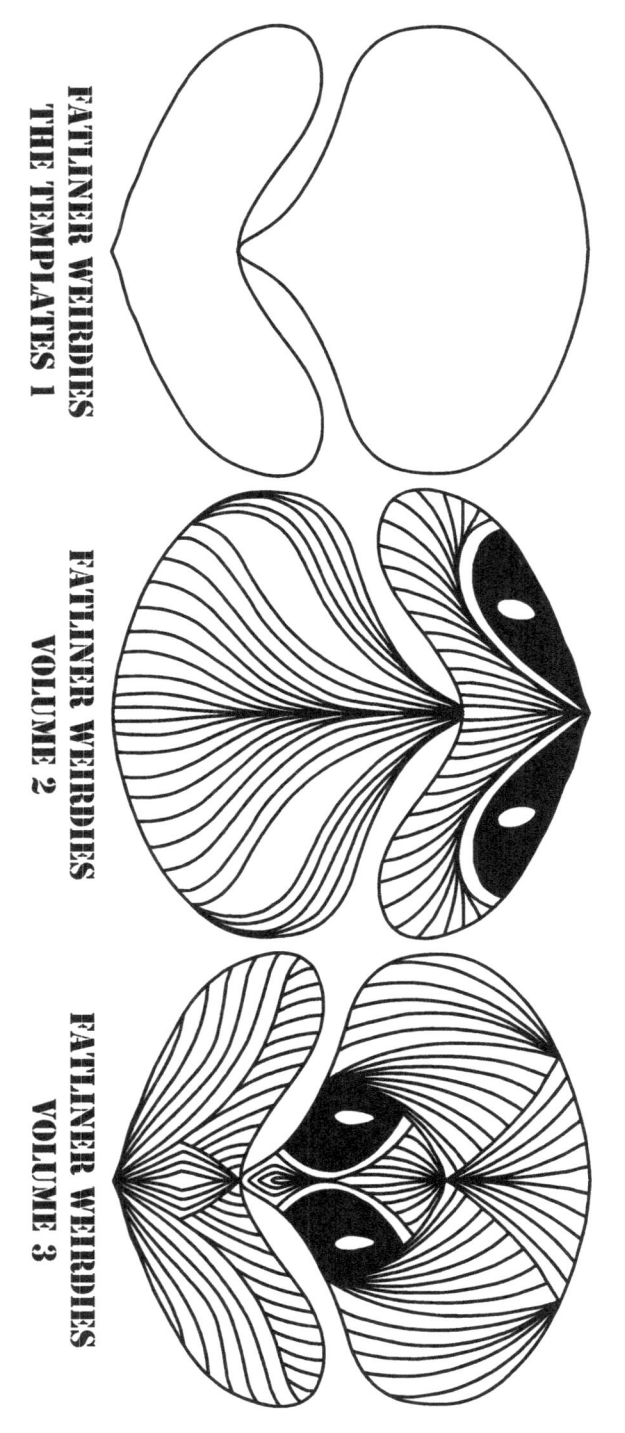

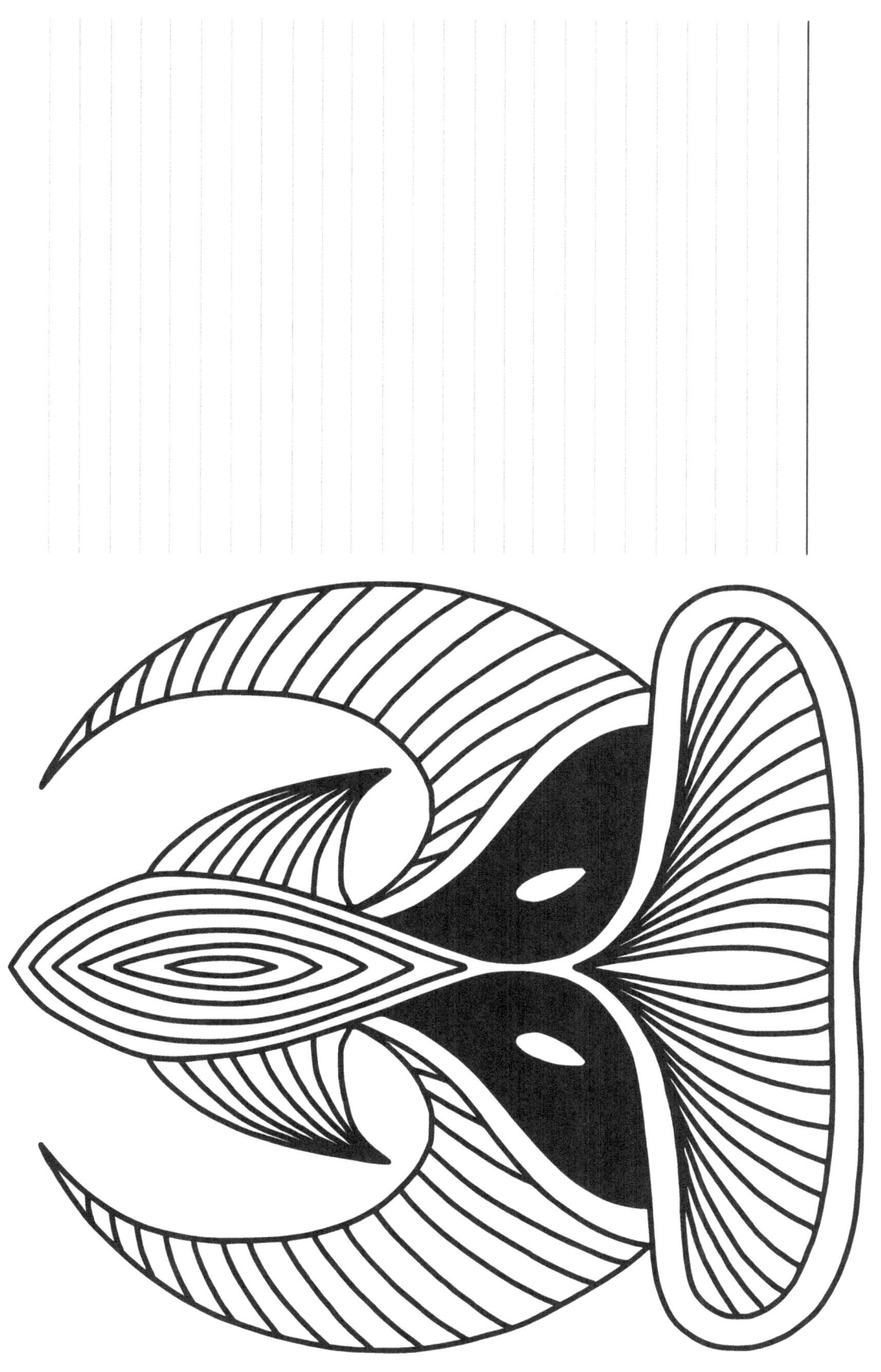

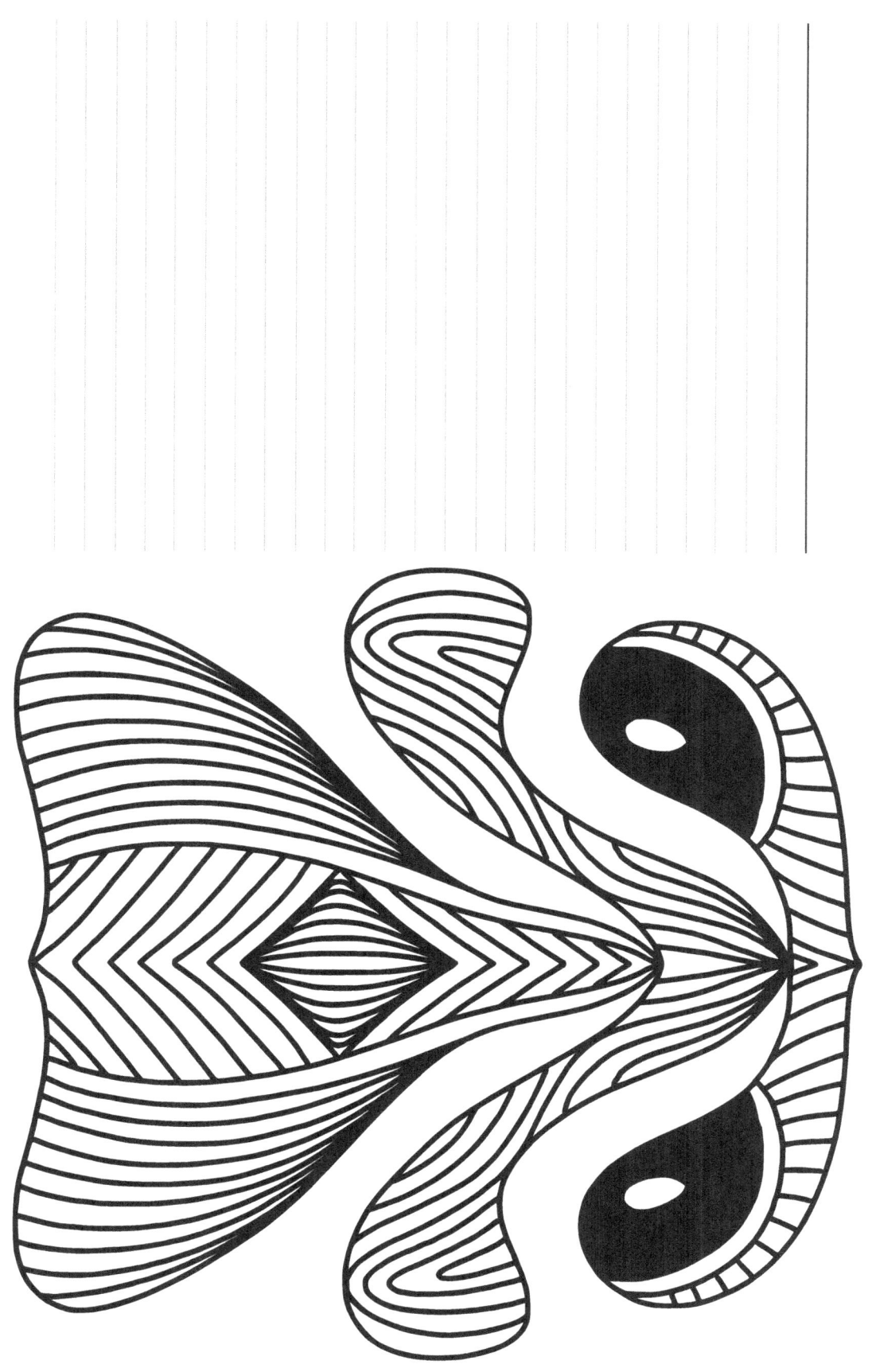

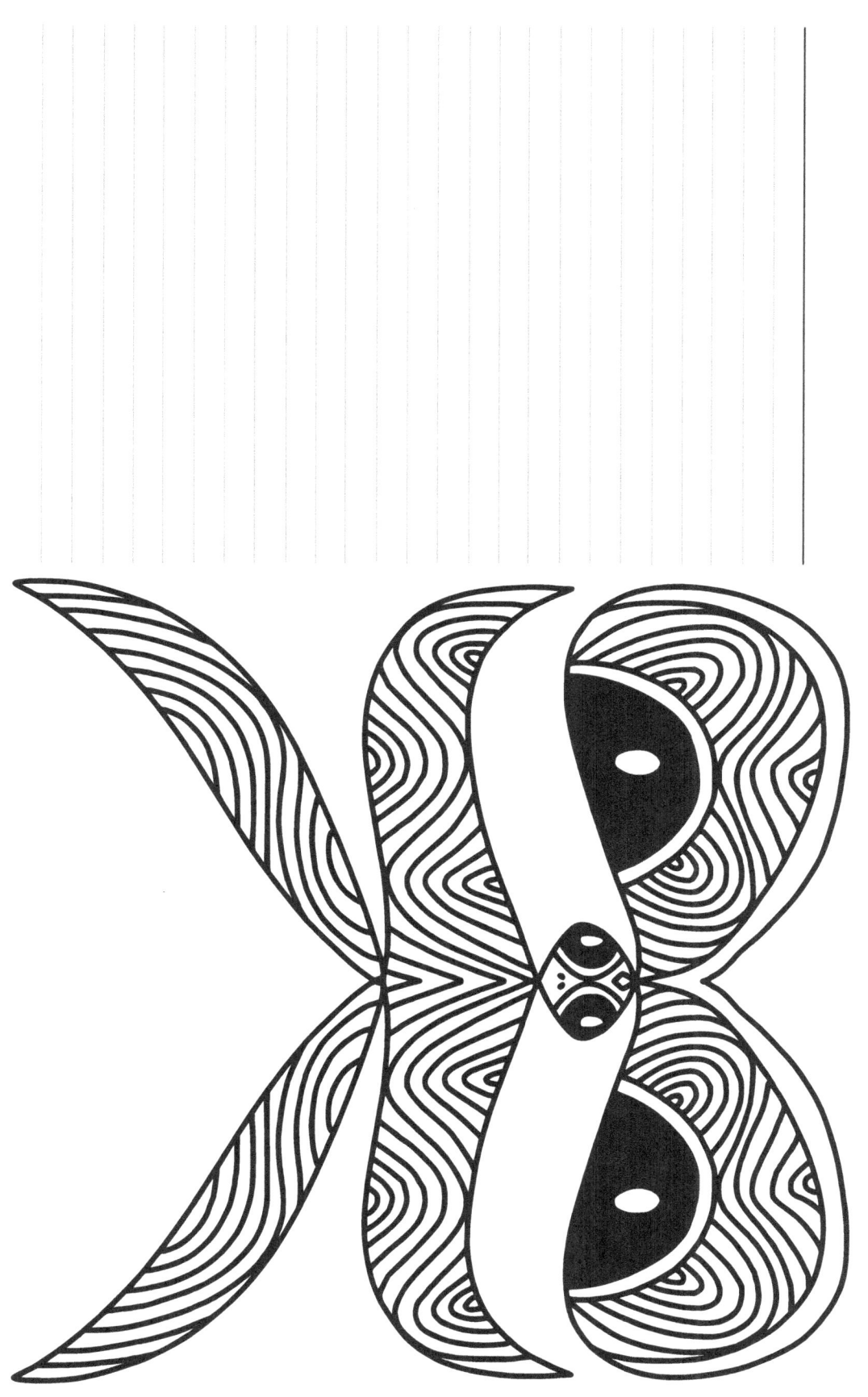

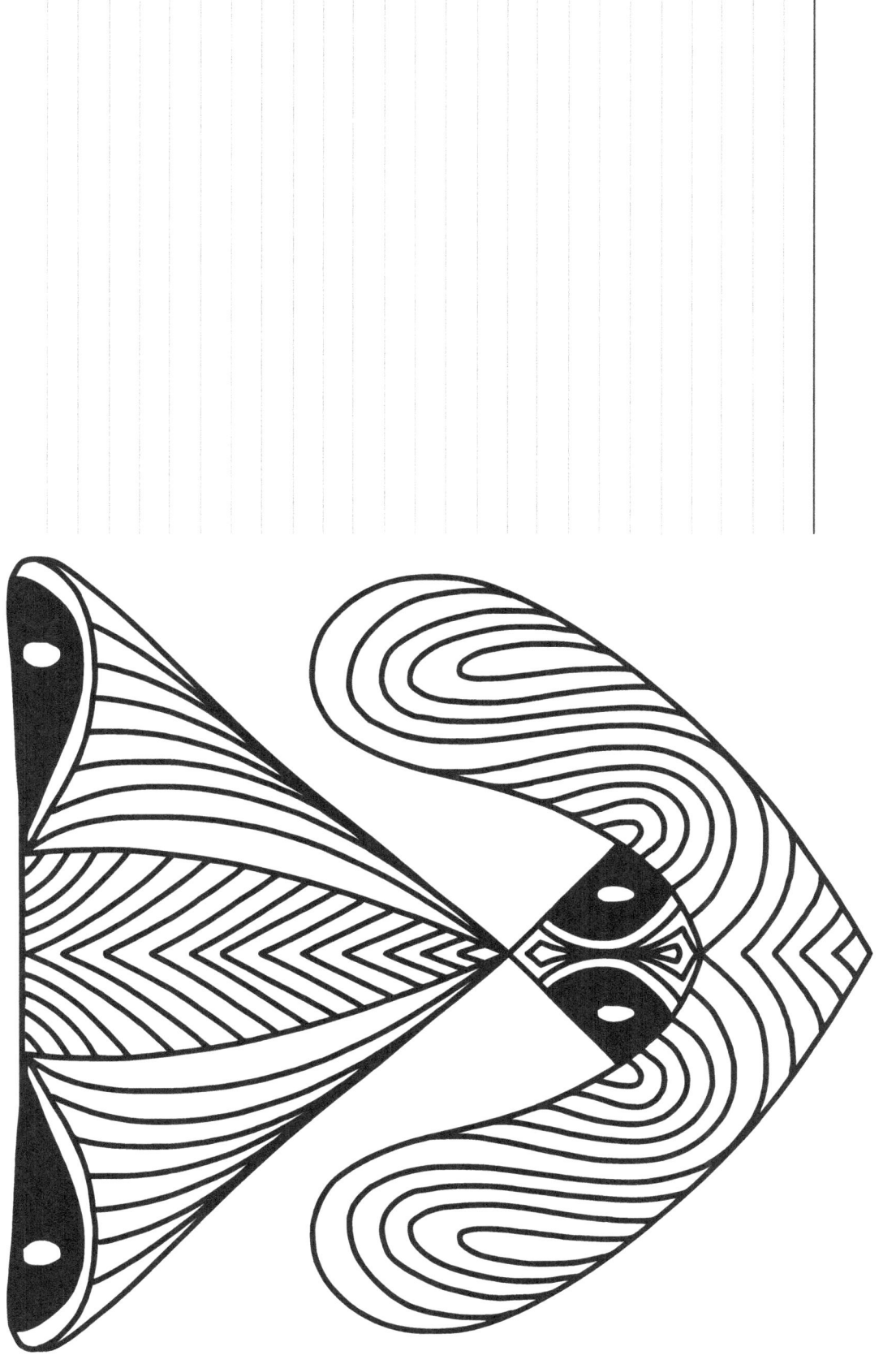

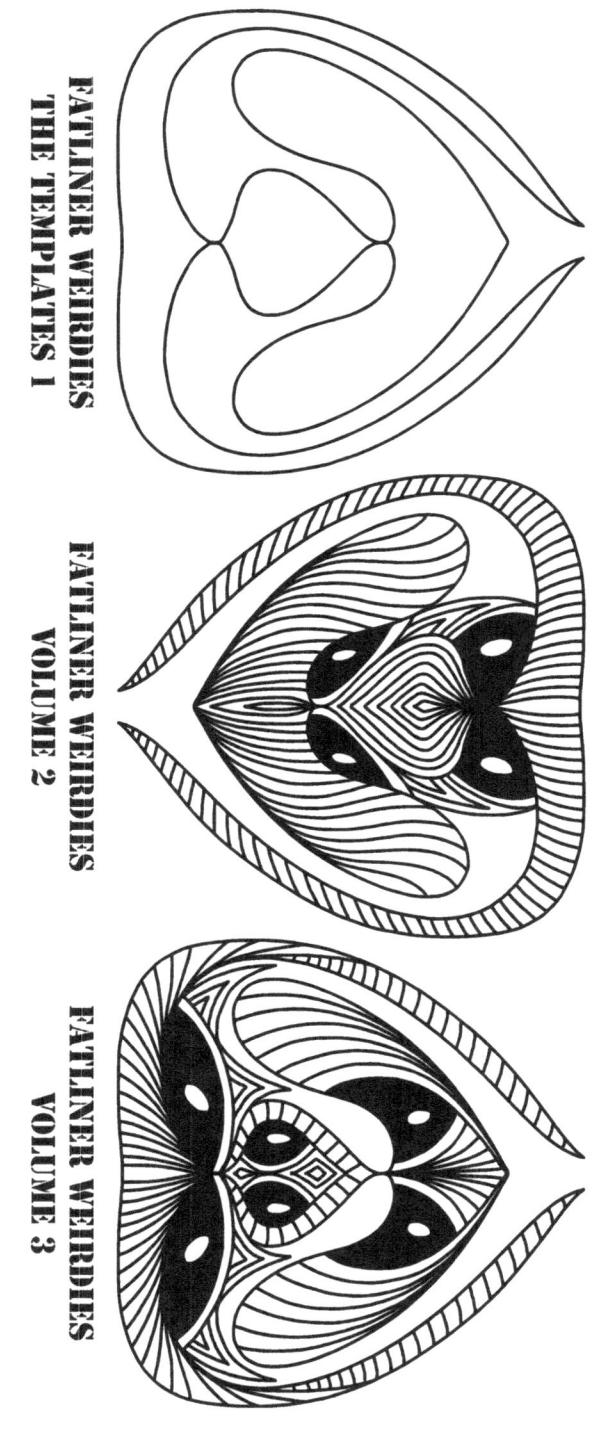

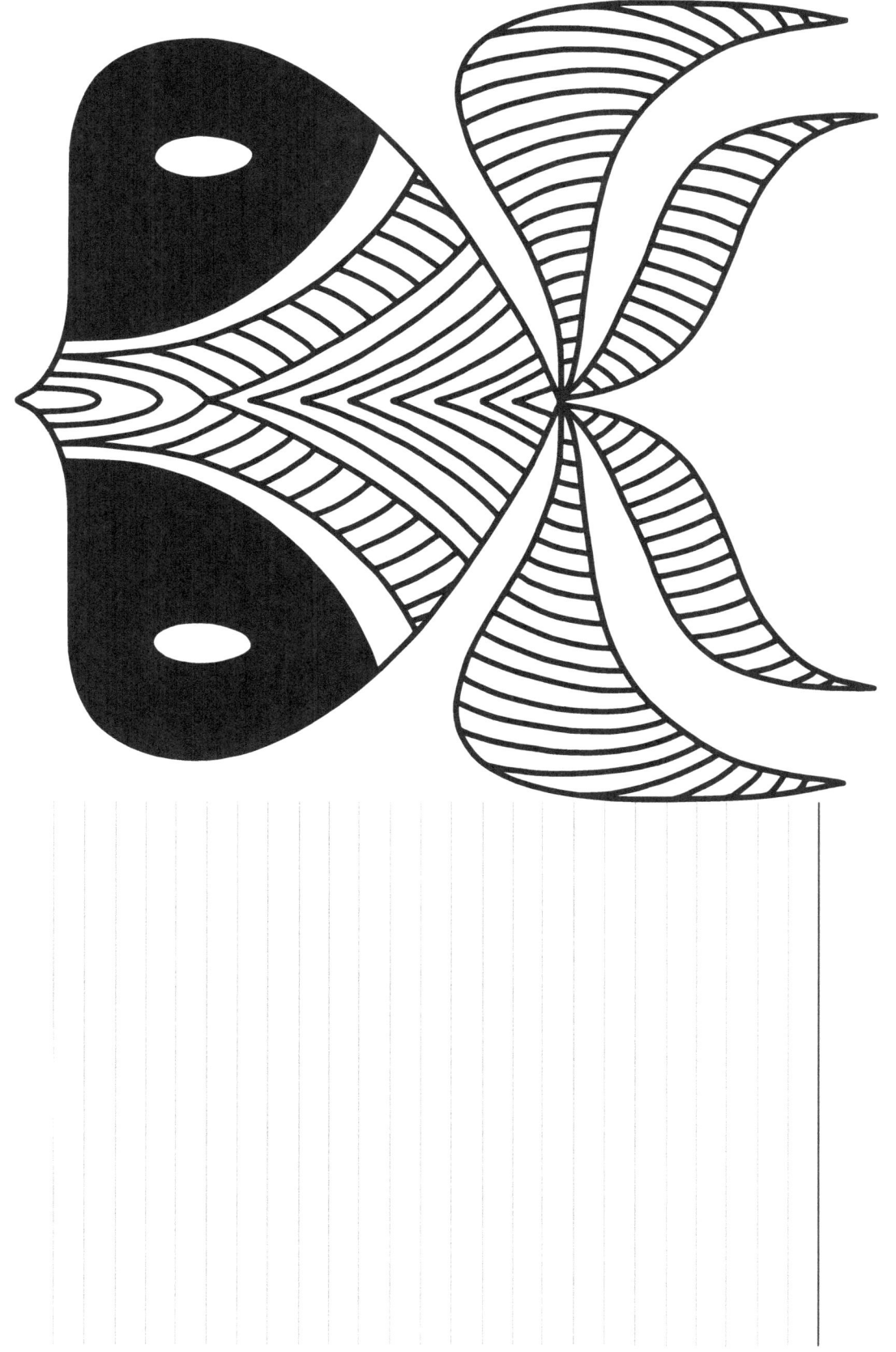

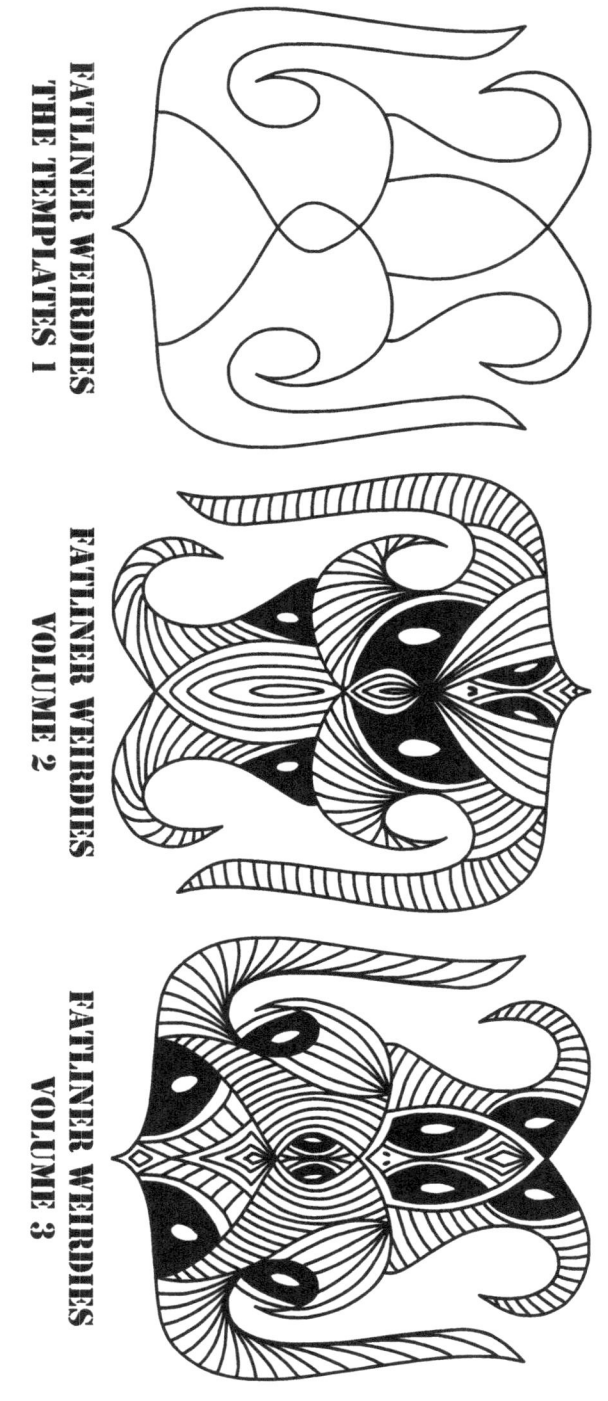

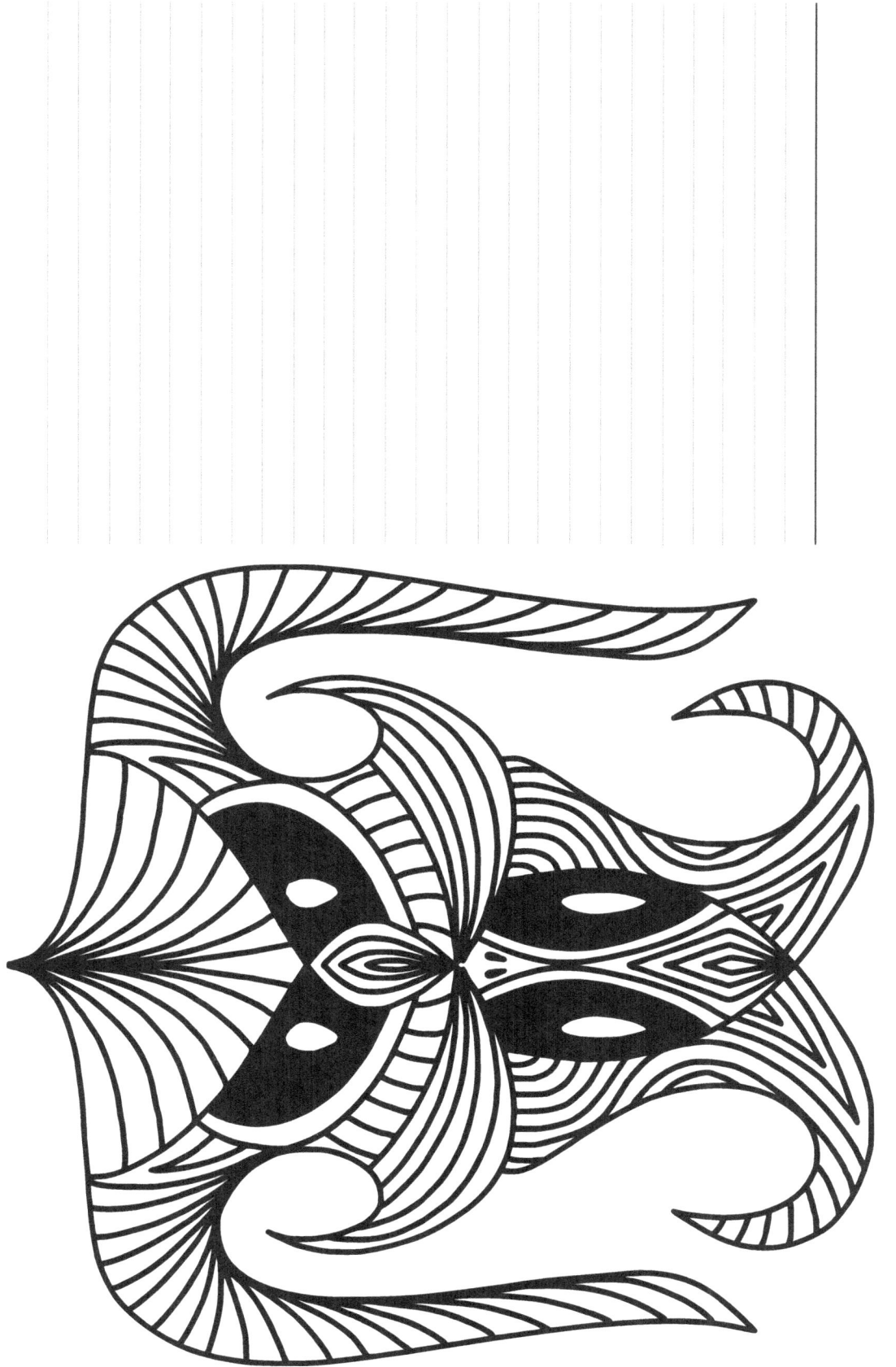

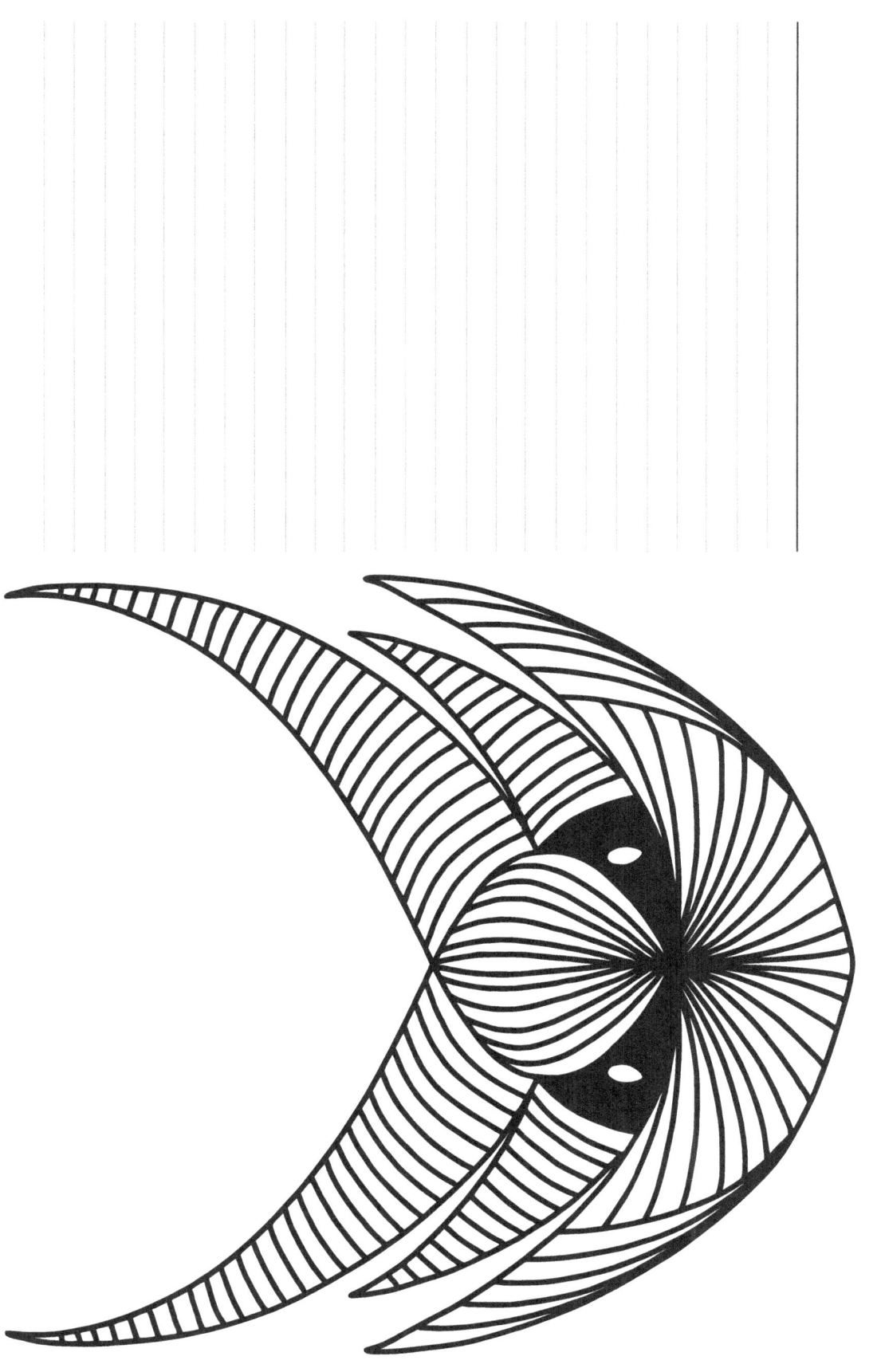

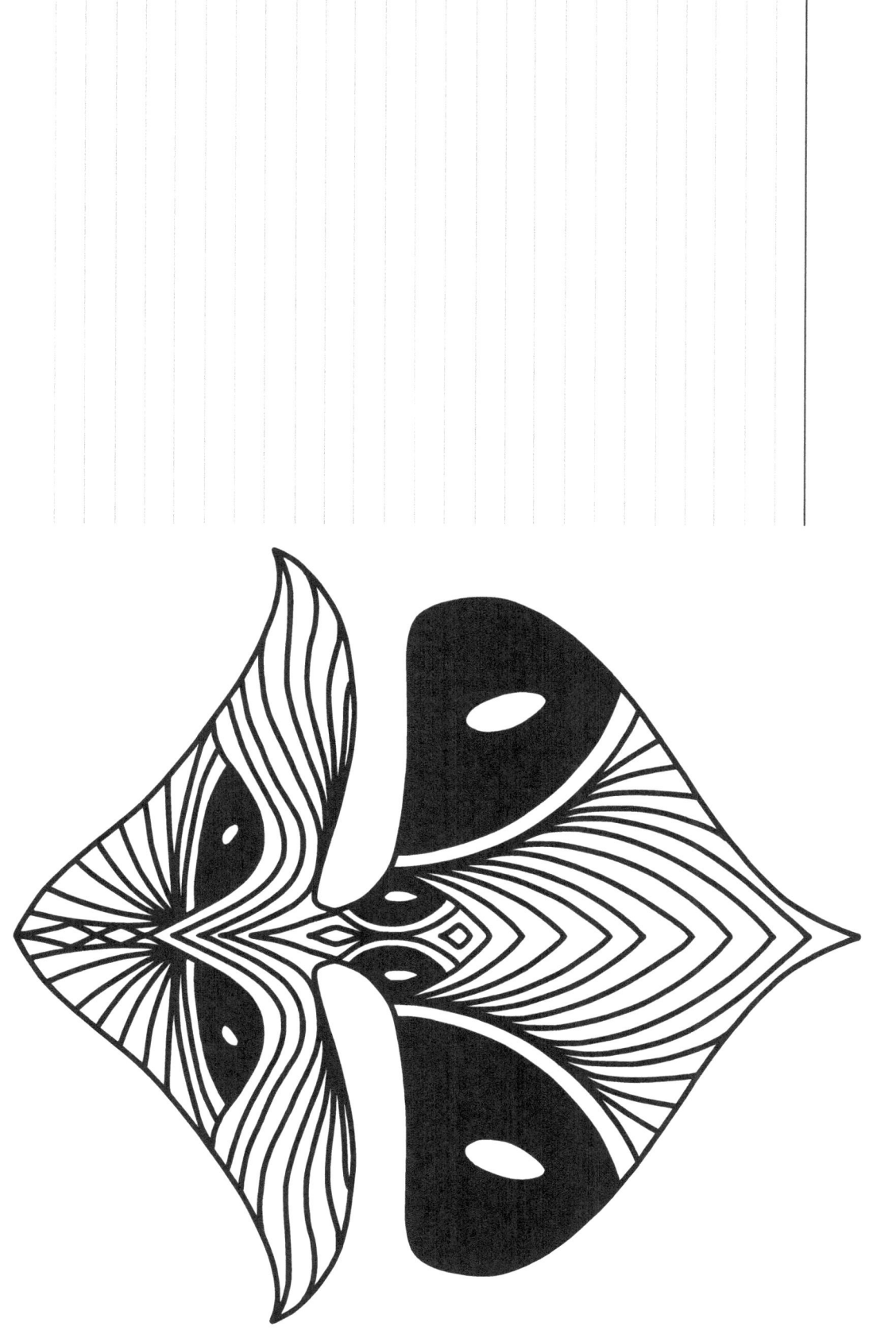

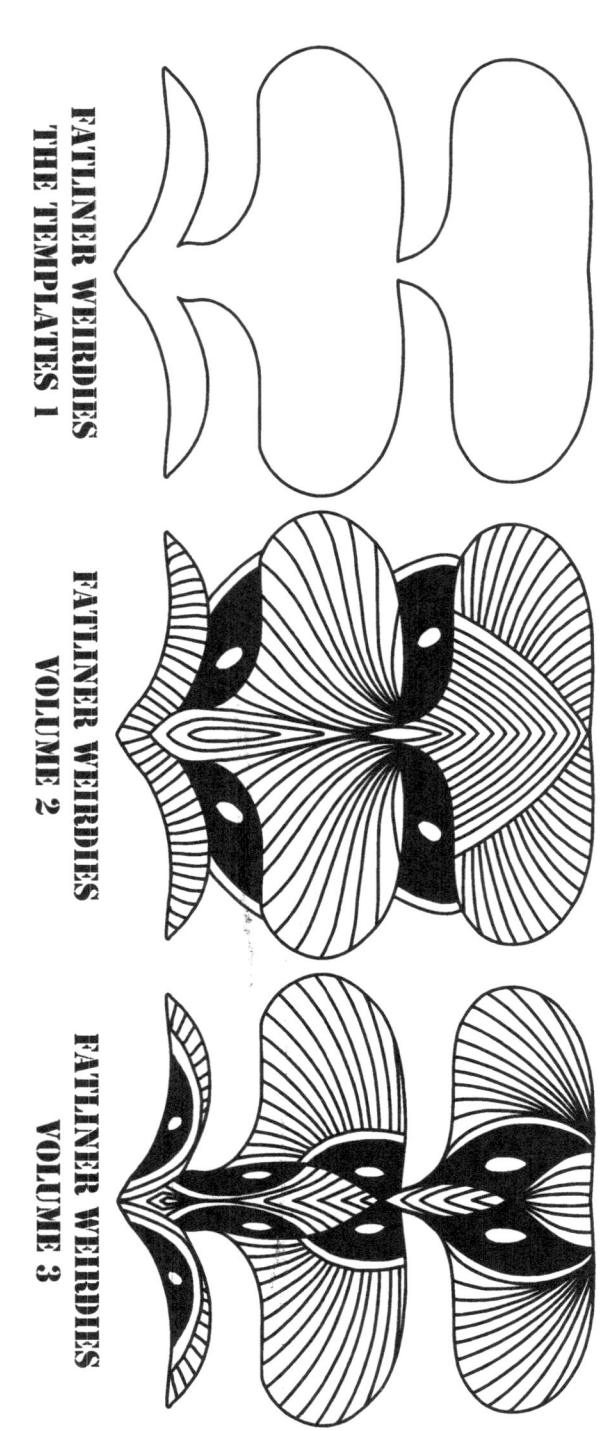

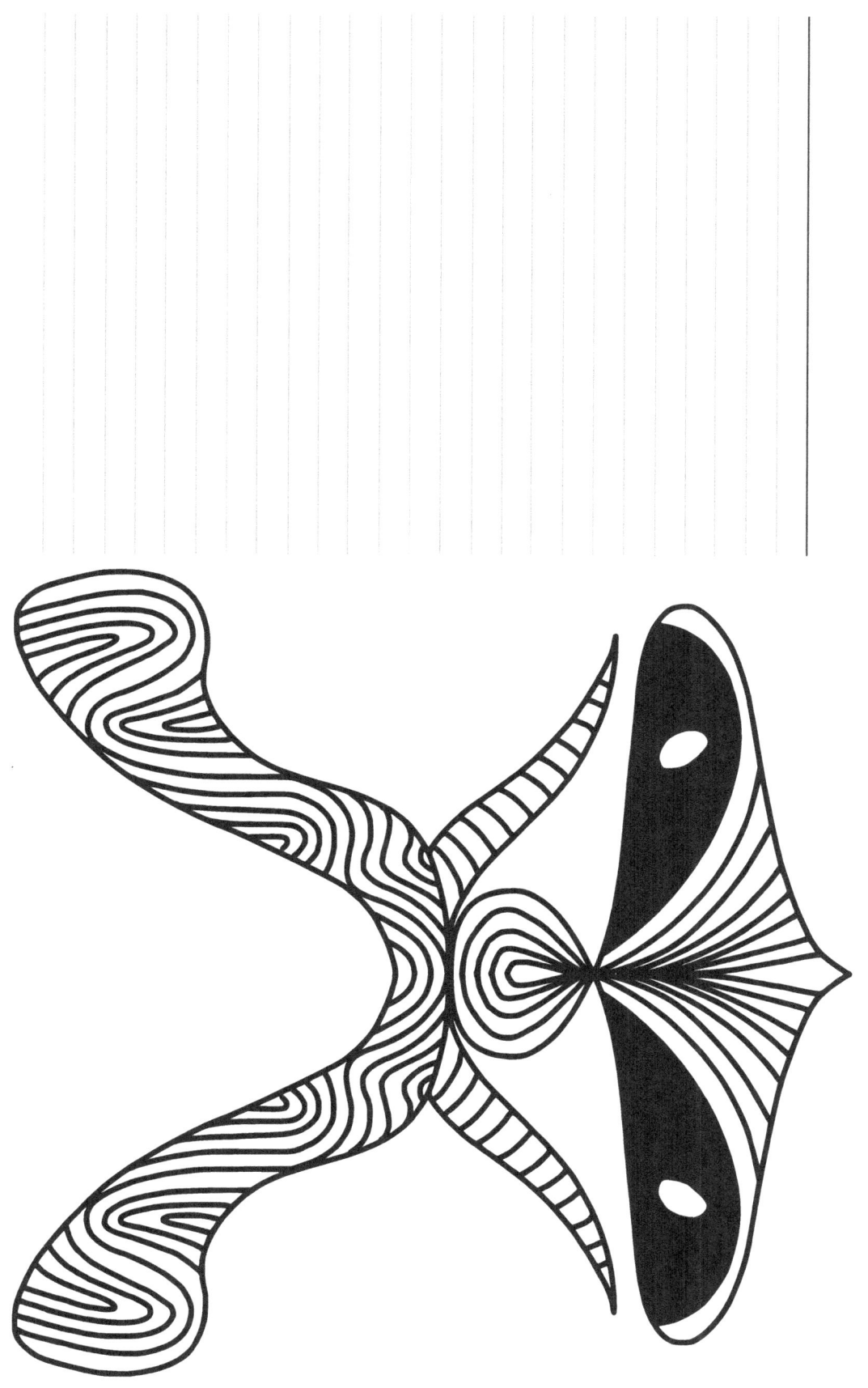

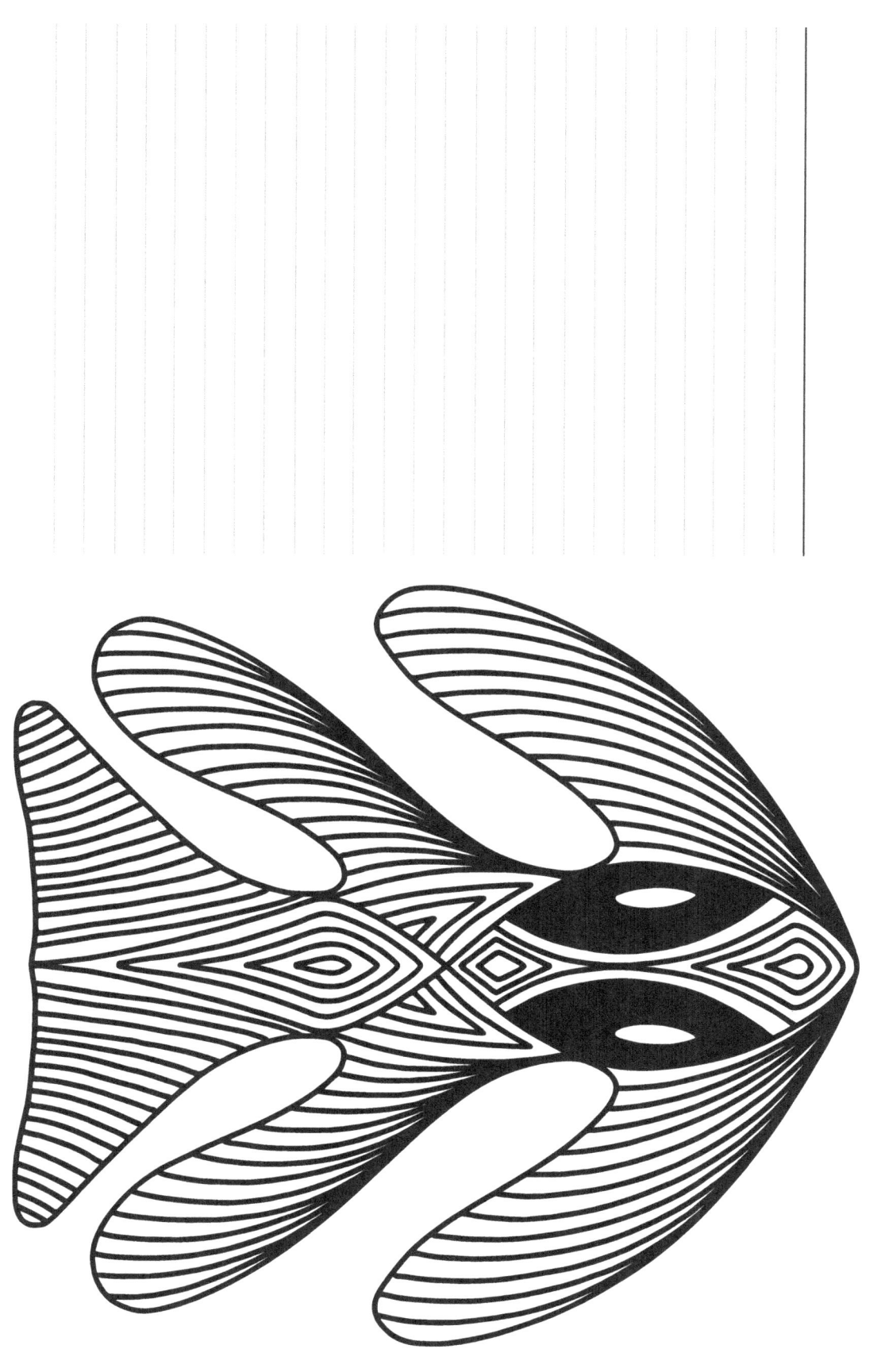

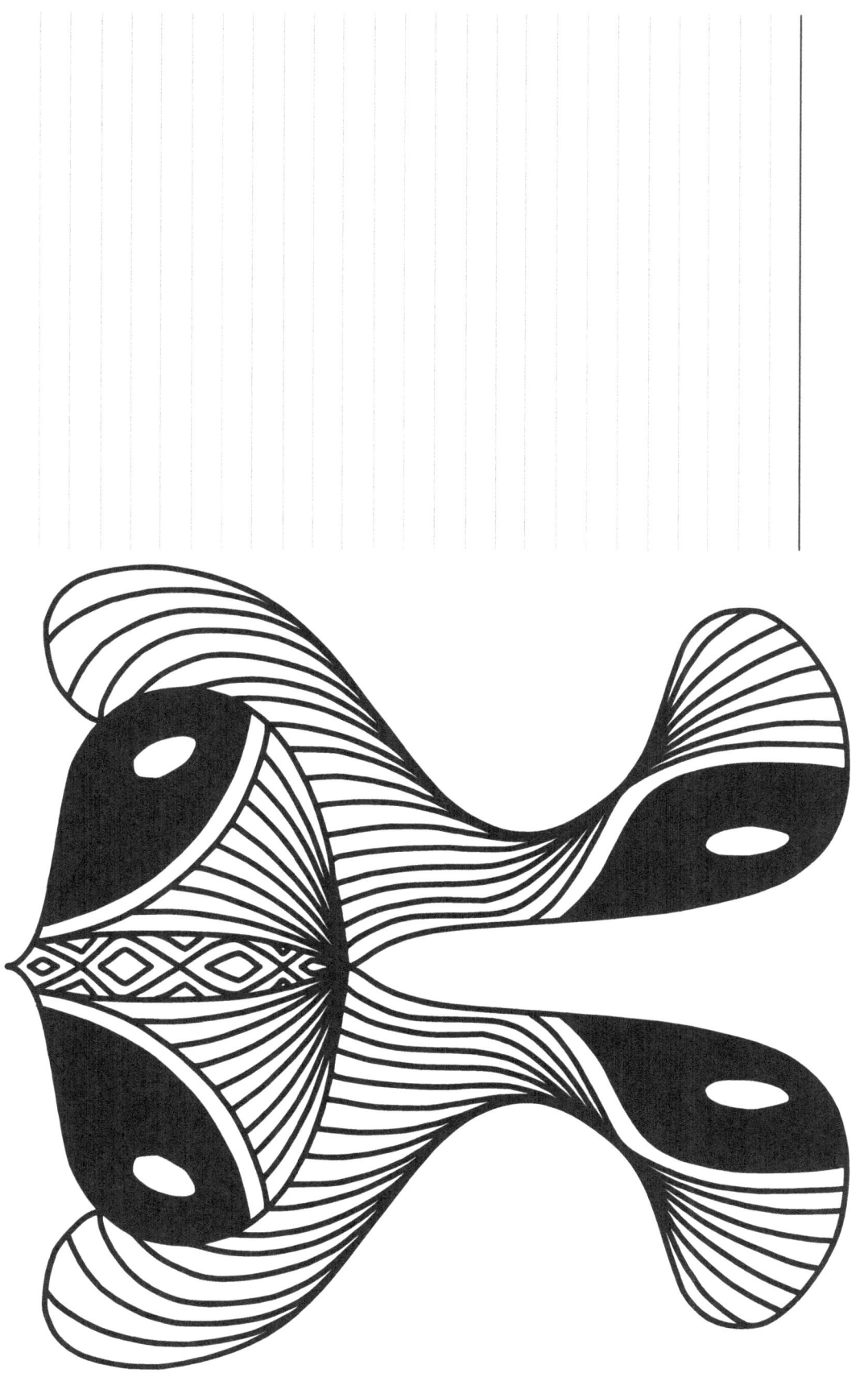

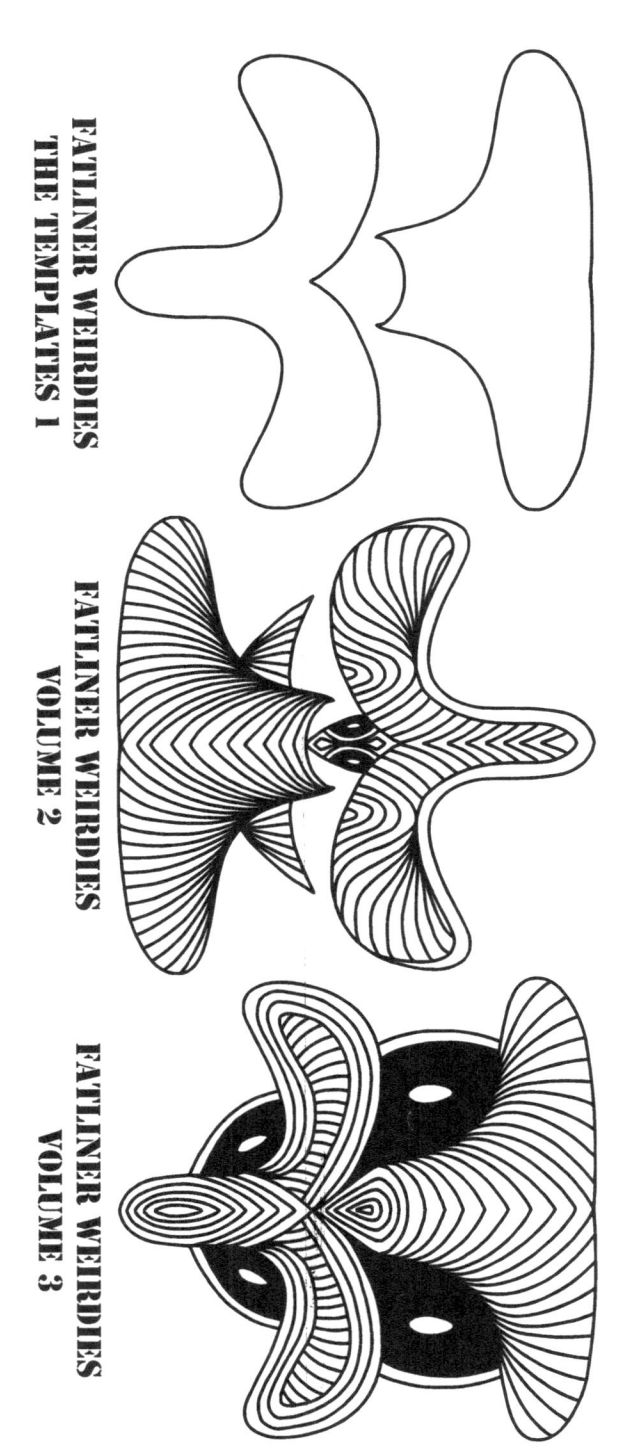

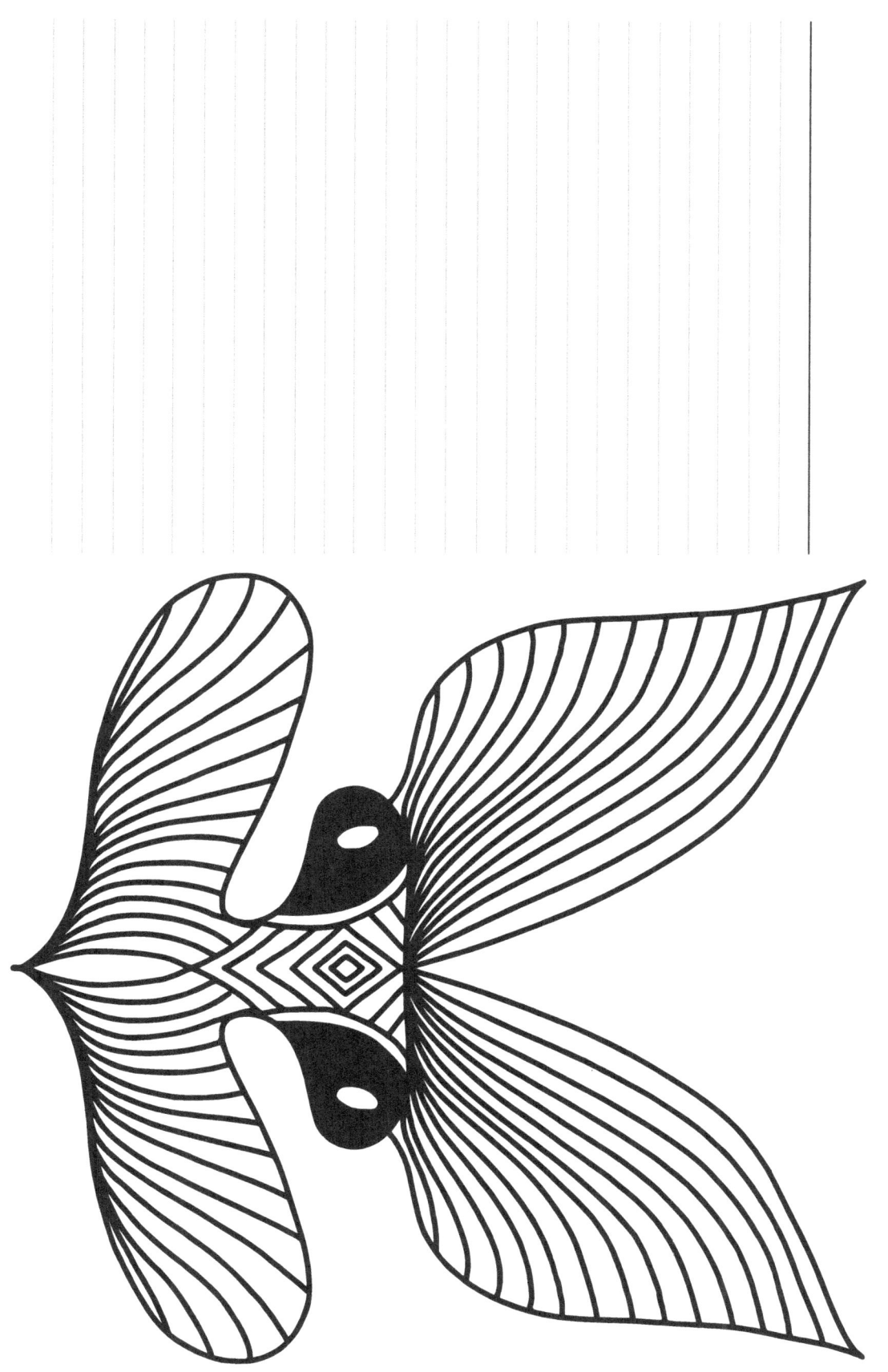

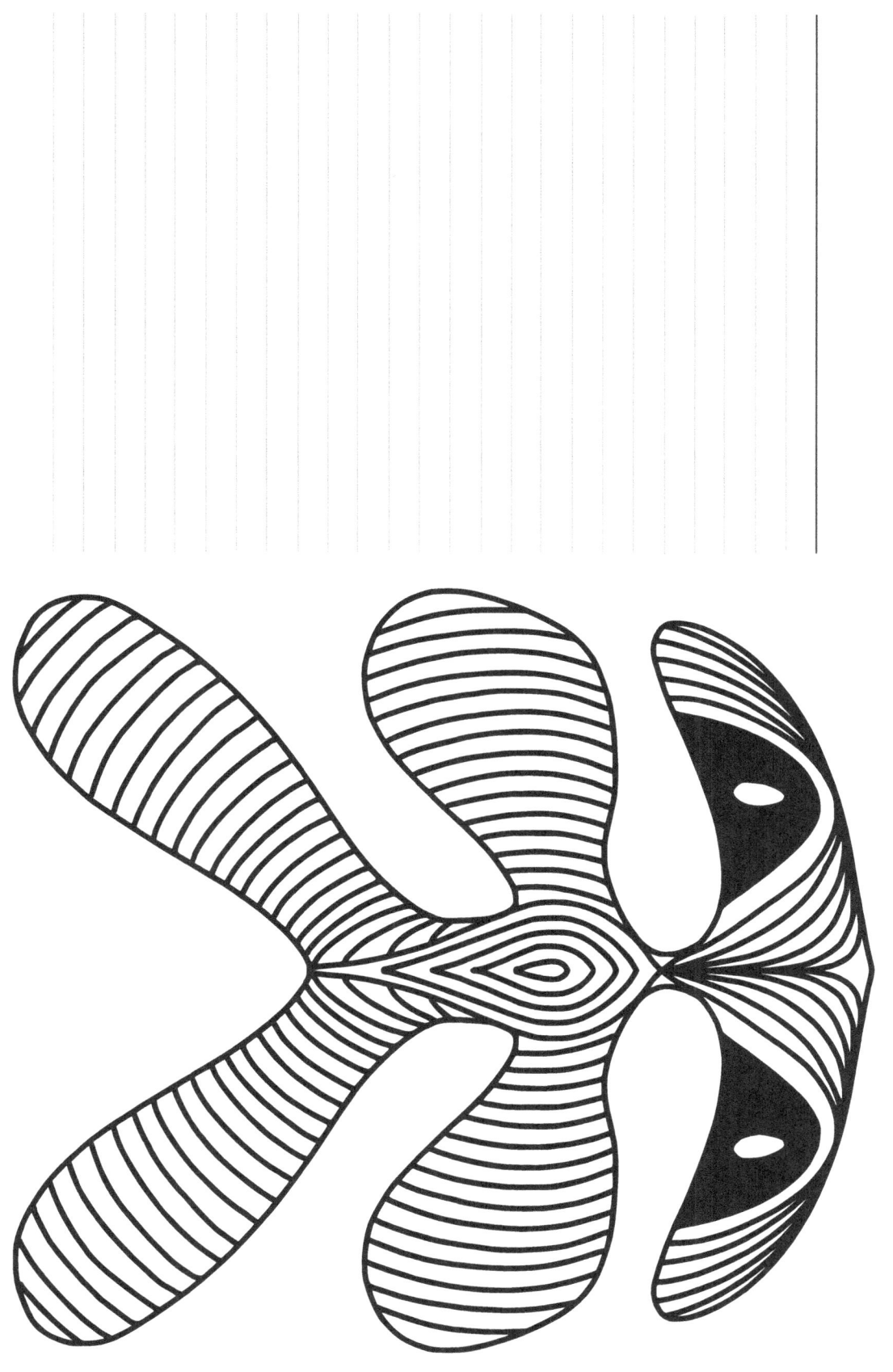

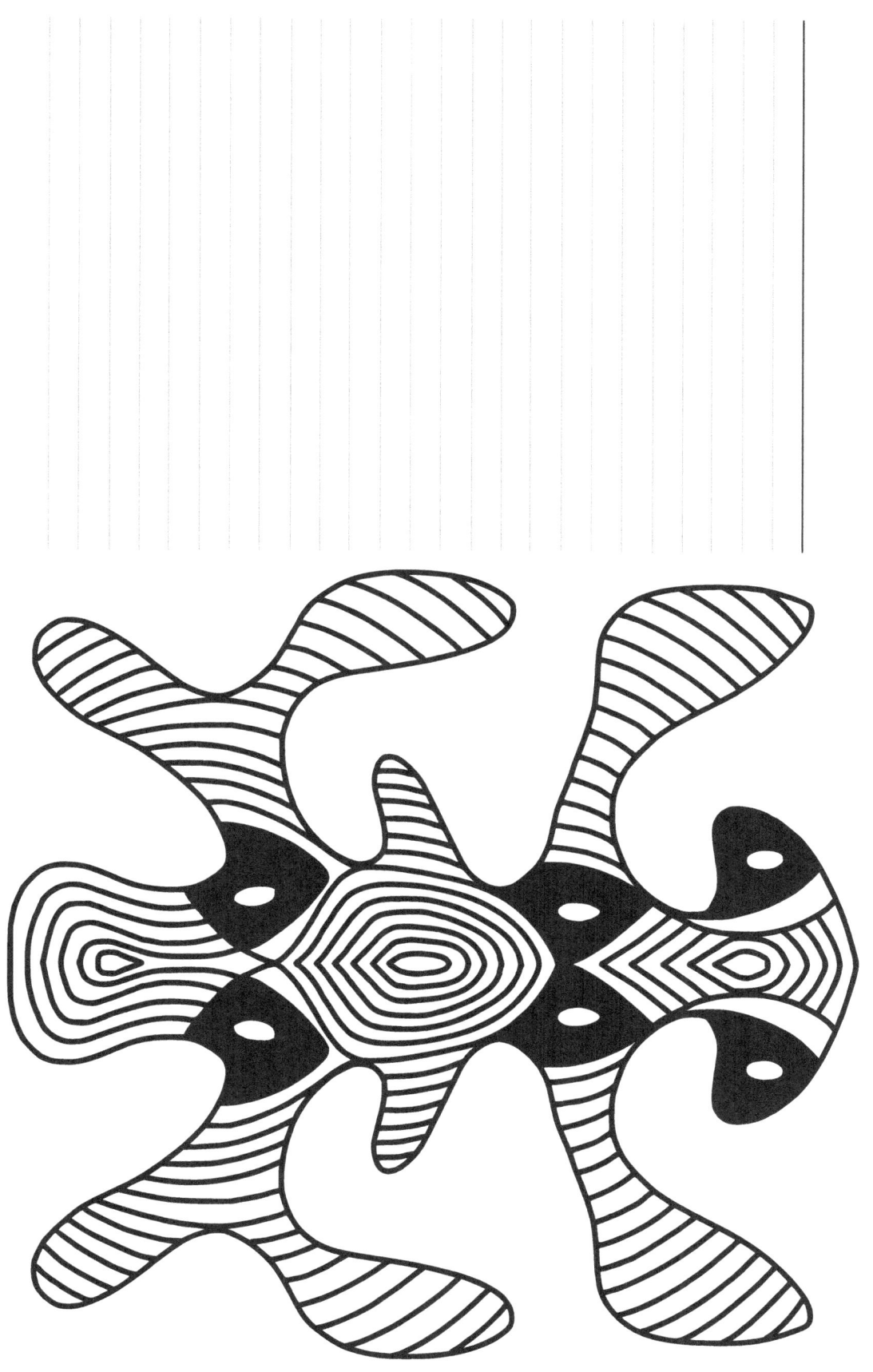

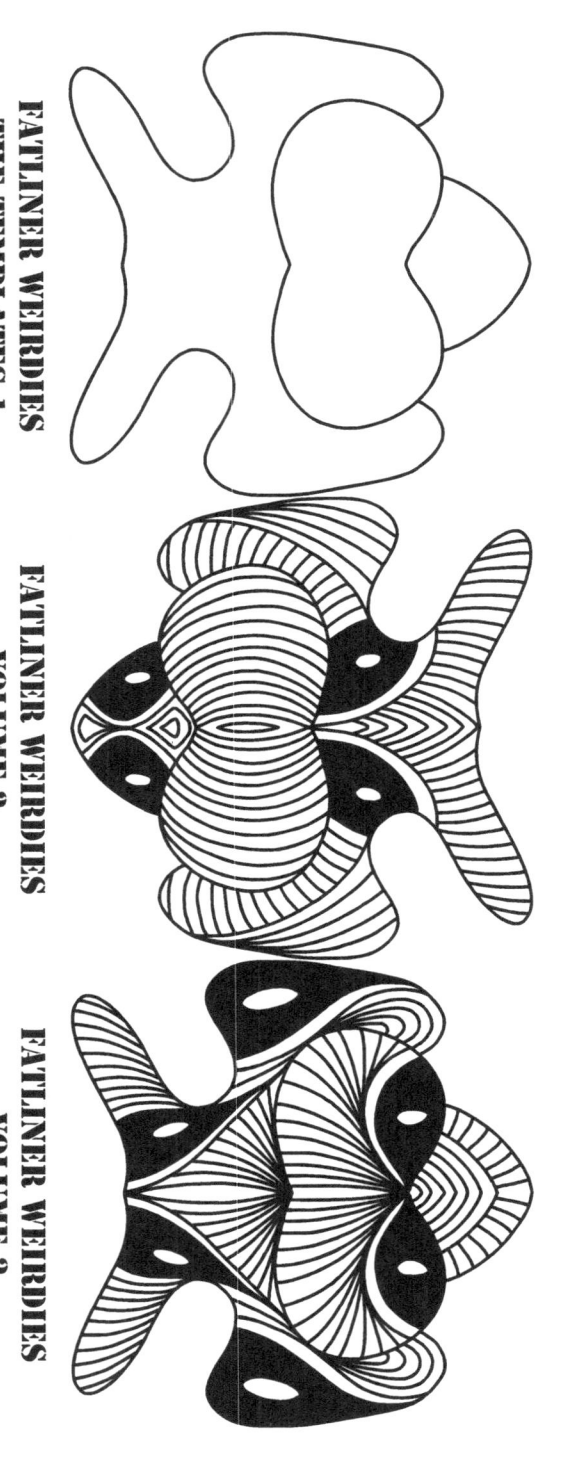

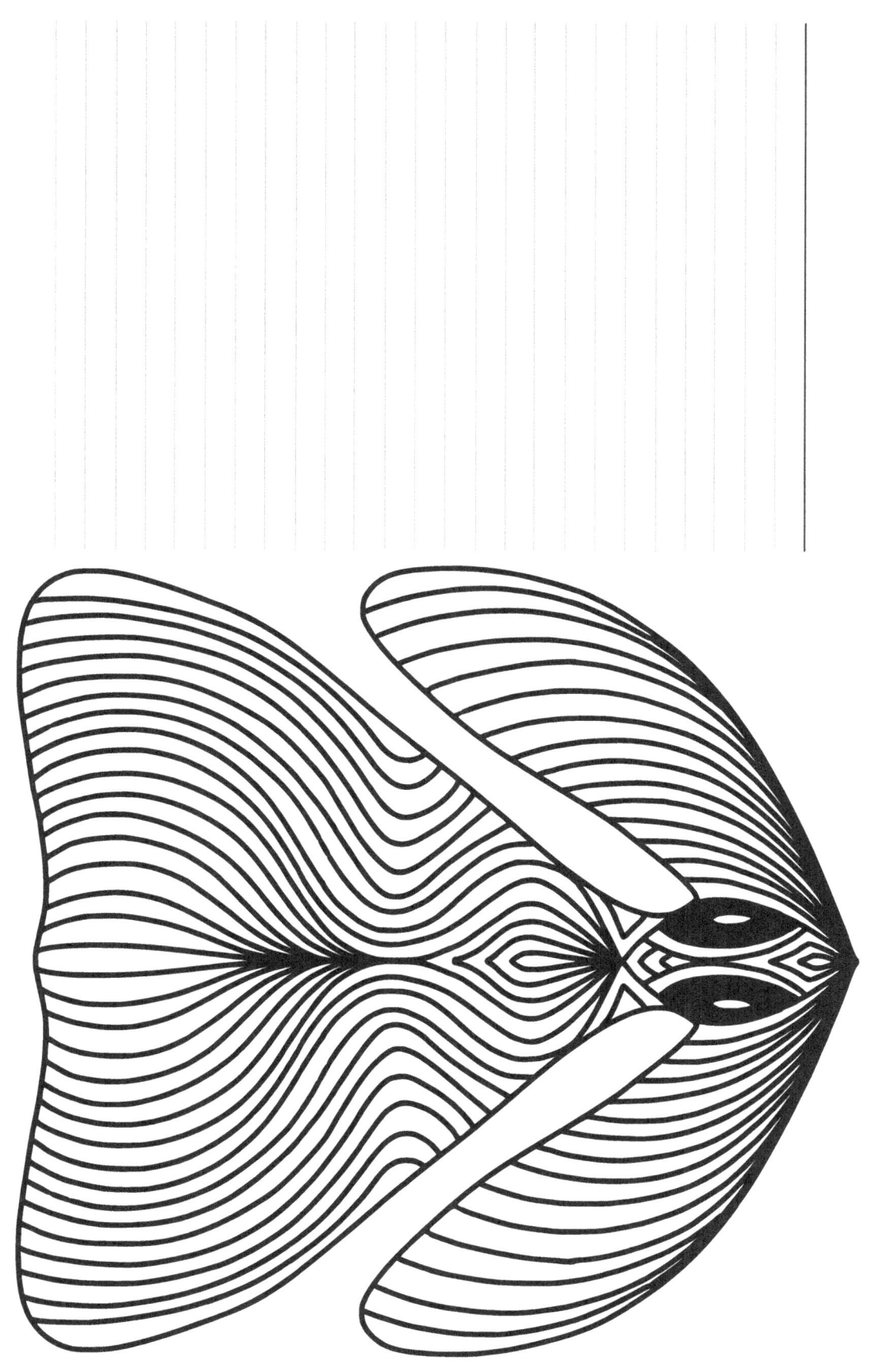

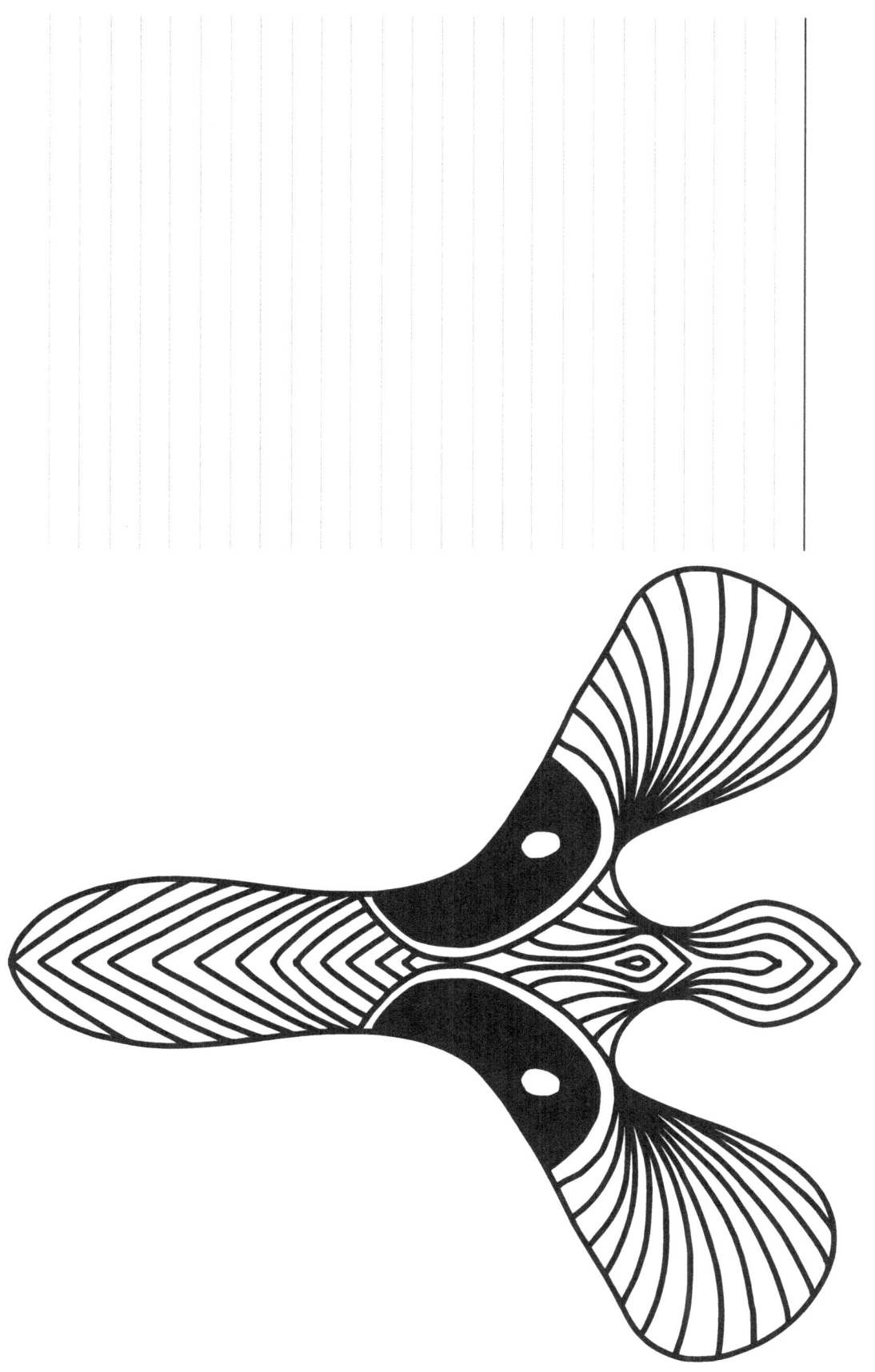

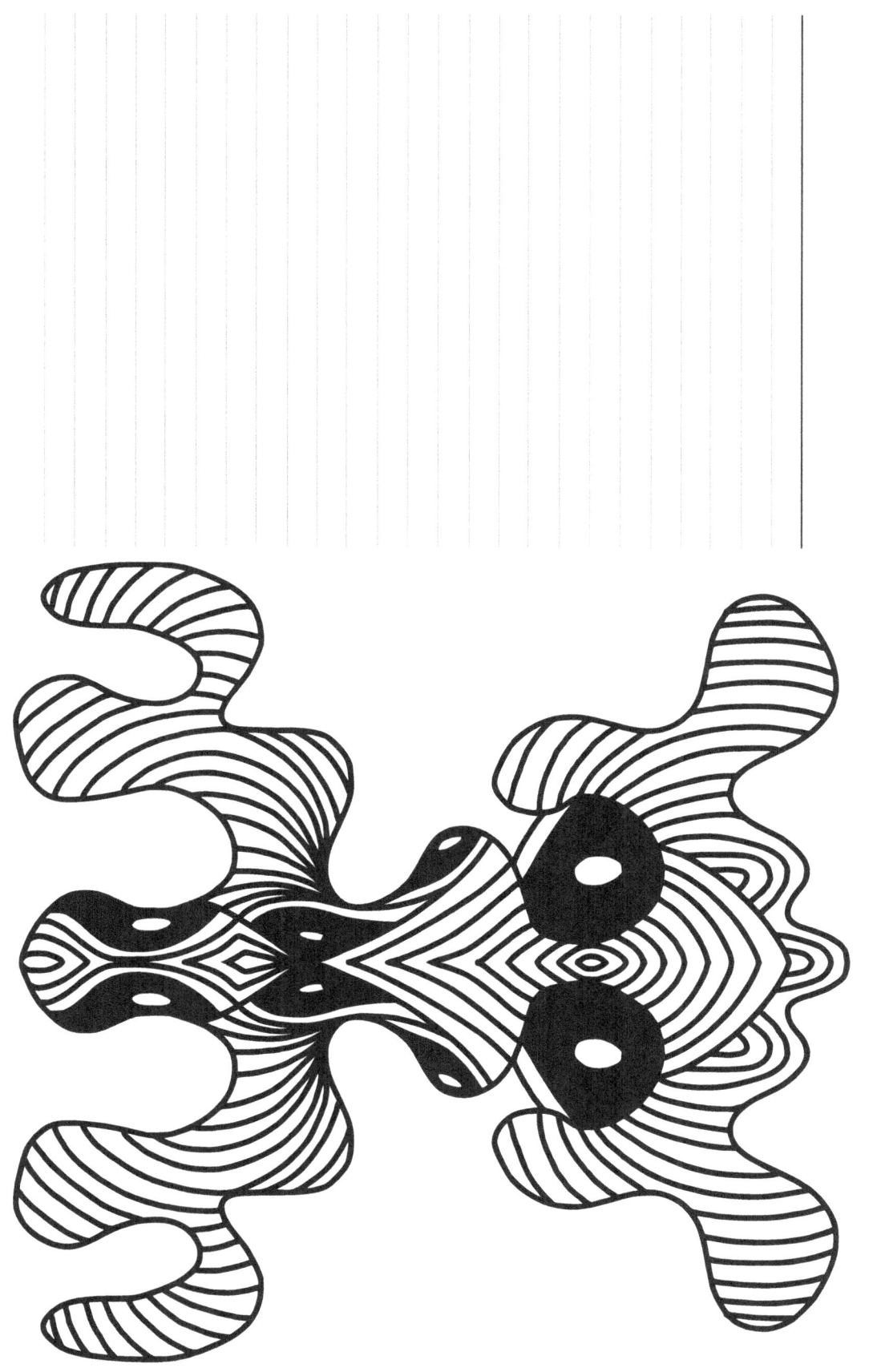

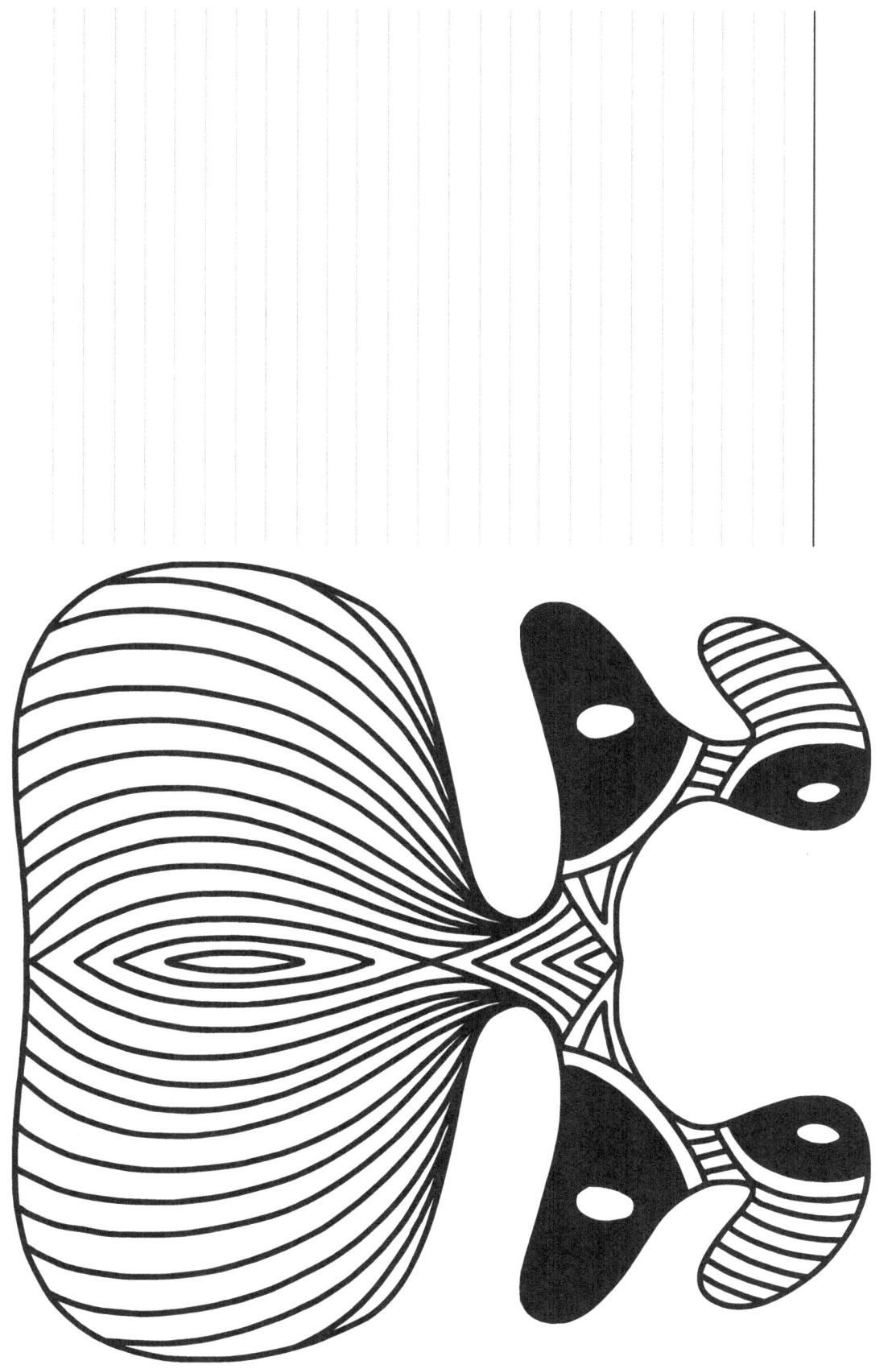

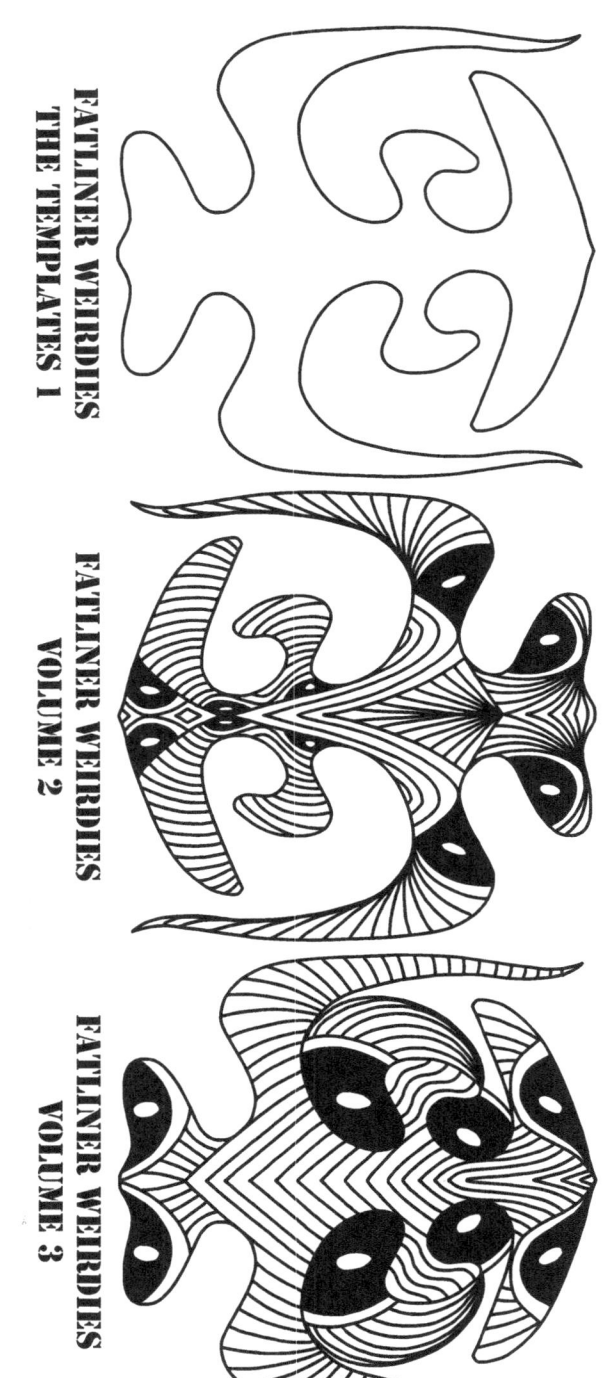

**FATLINER WEIRDIES
THE TEMPLATES 1**

**FATLINER WEIRDIES
VOLUME 2**

**FATLINER WEIRDIES
VOLUME 3**

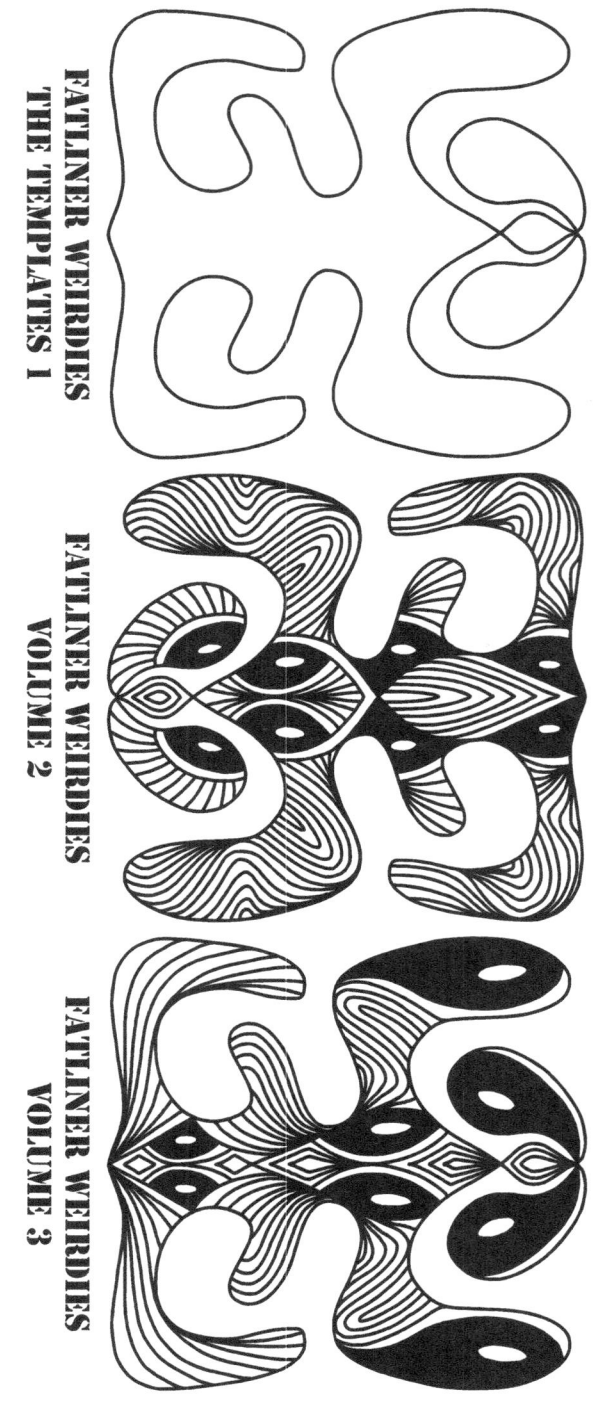

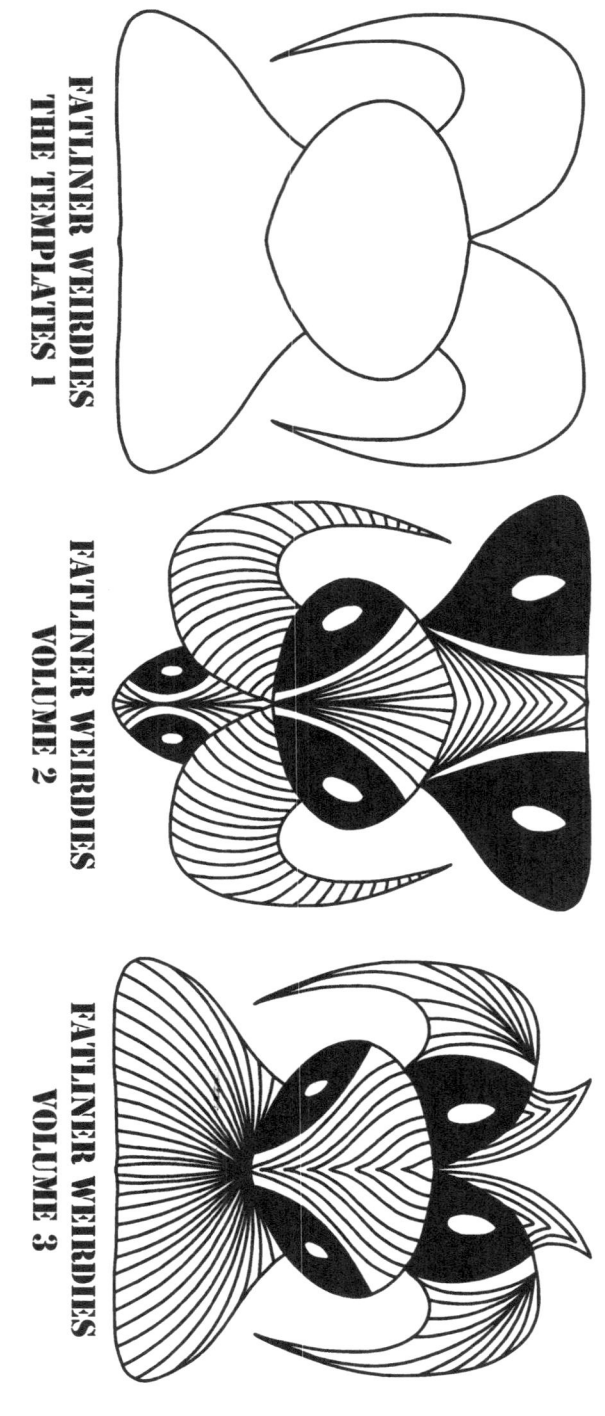

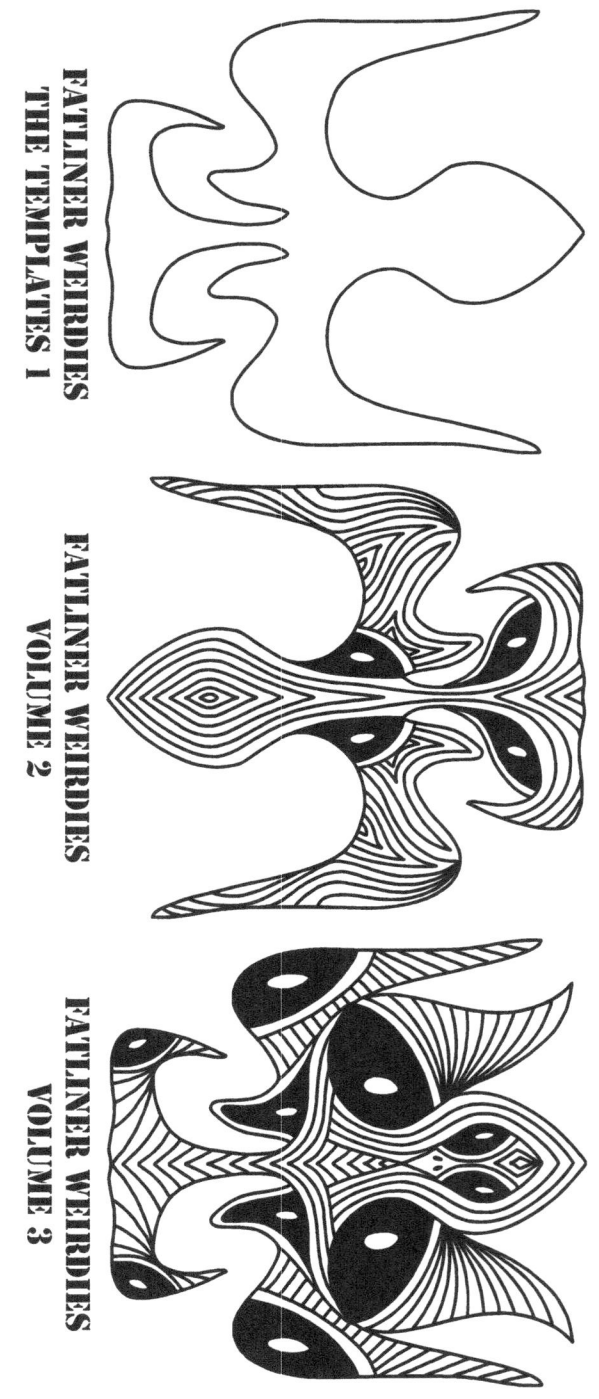

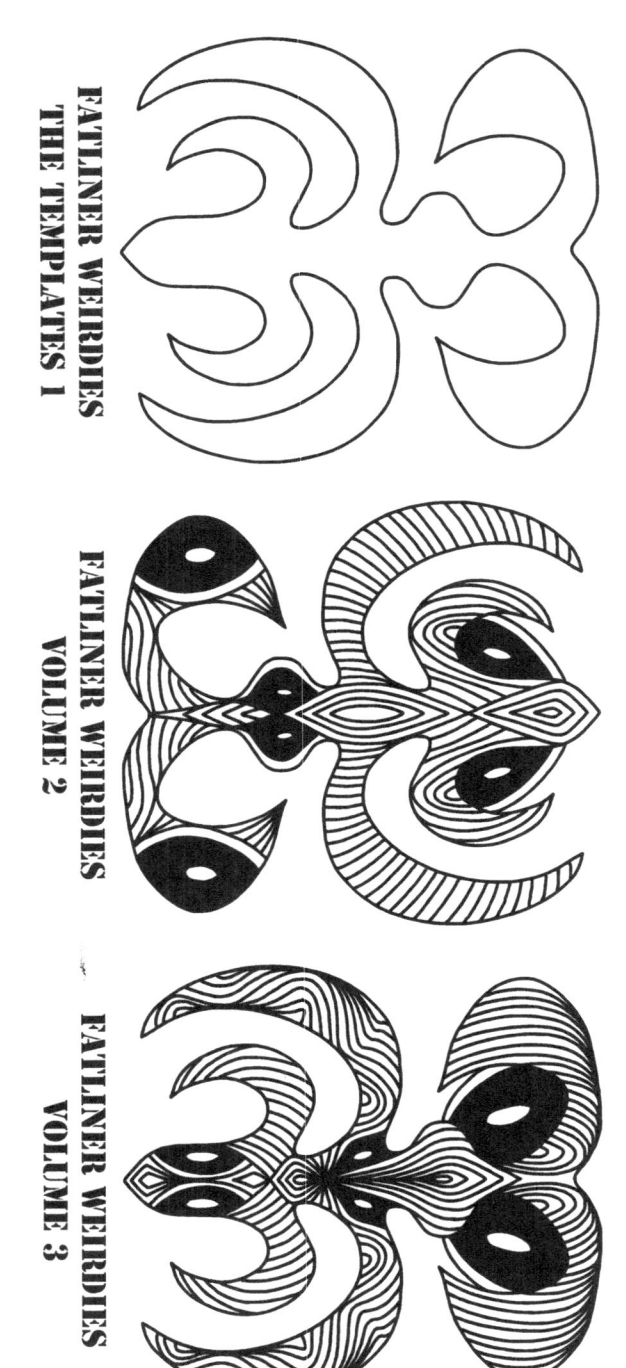

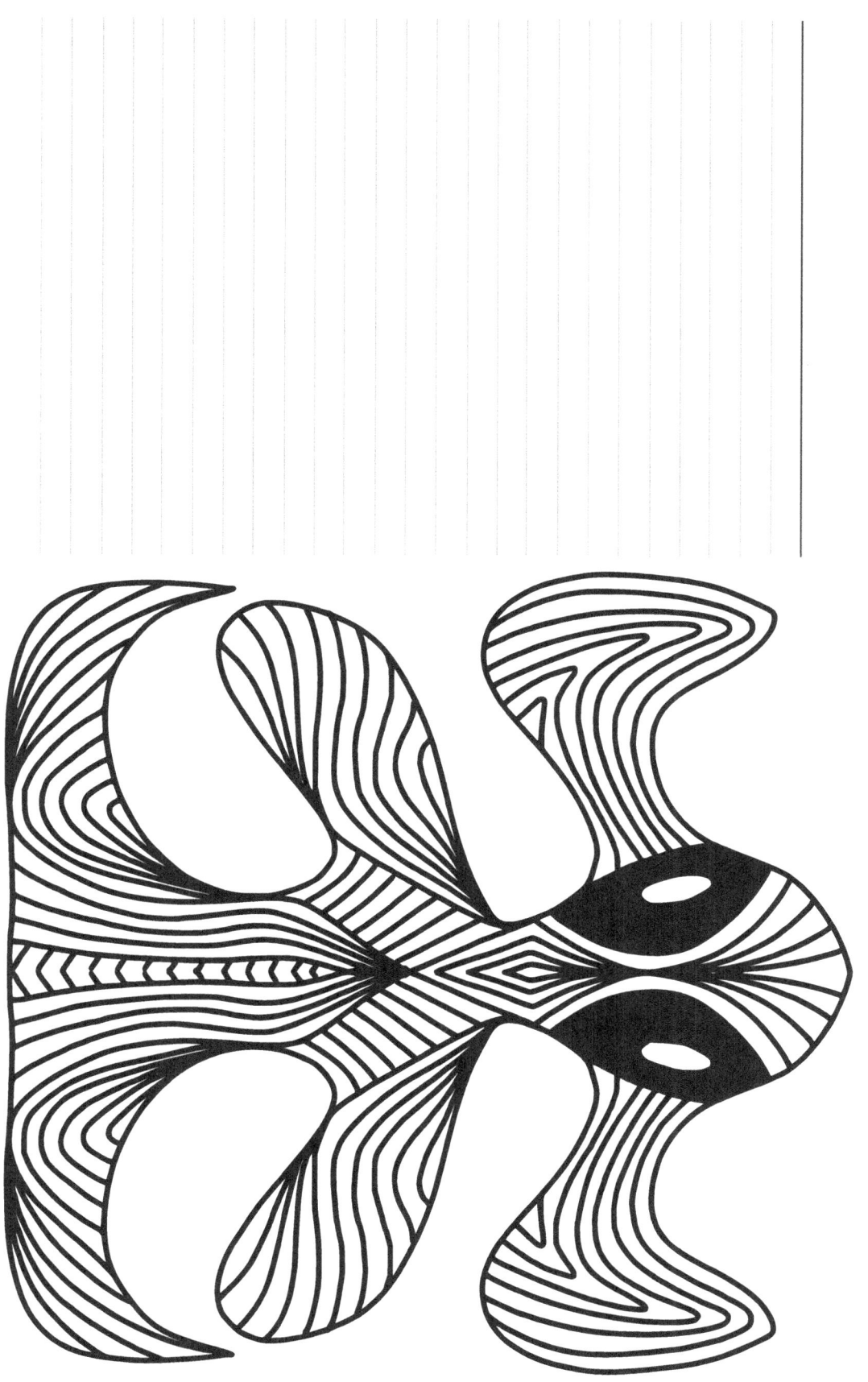

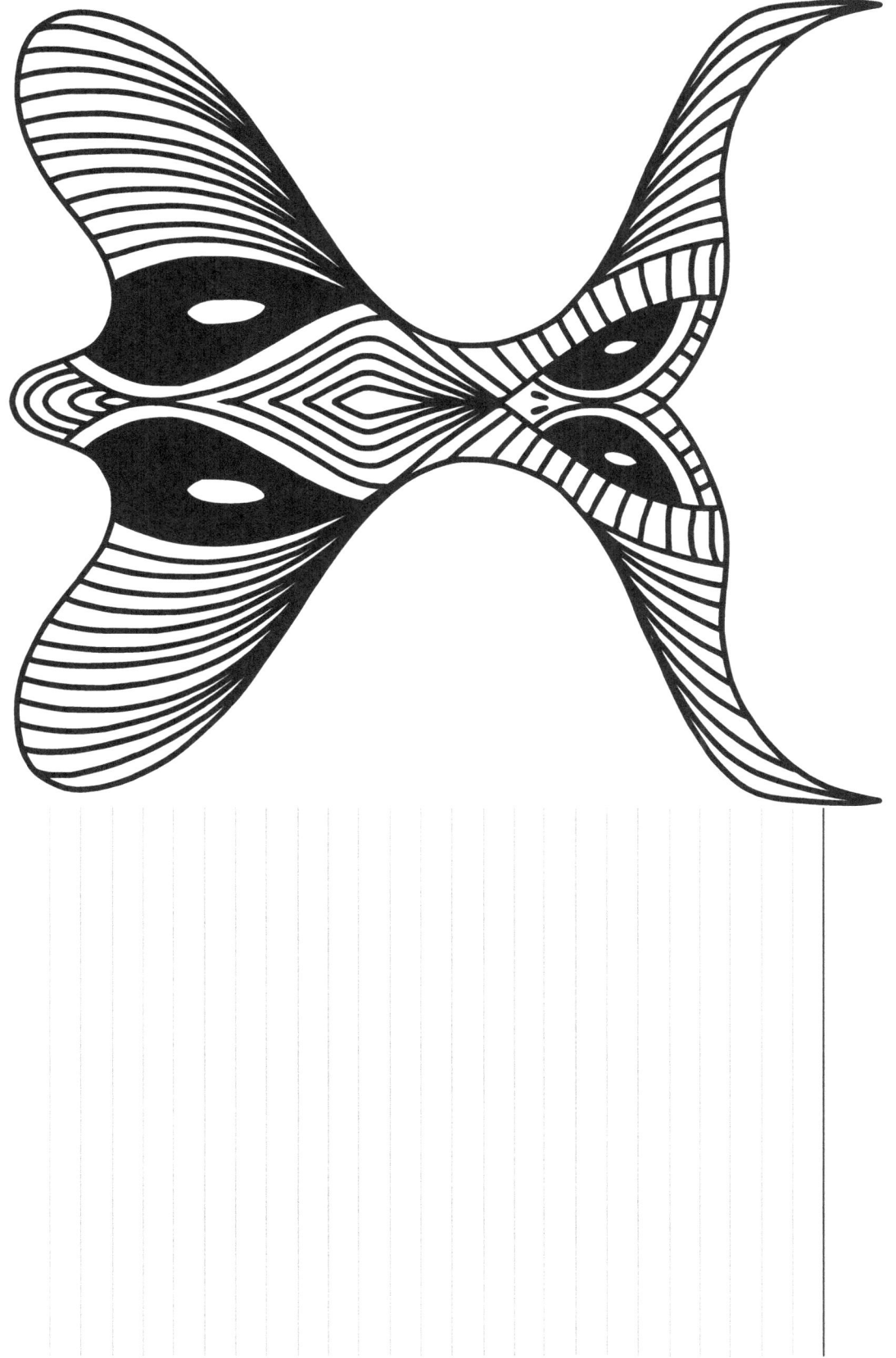

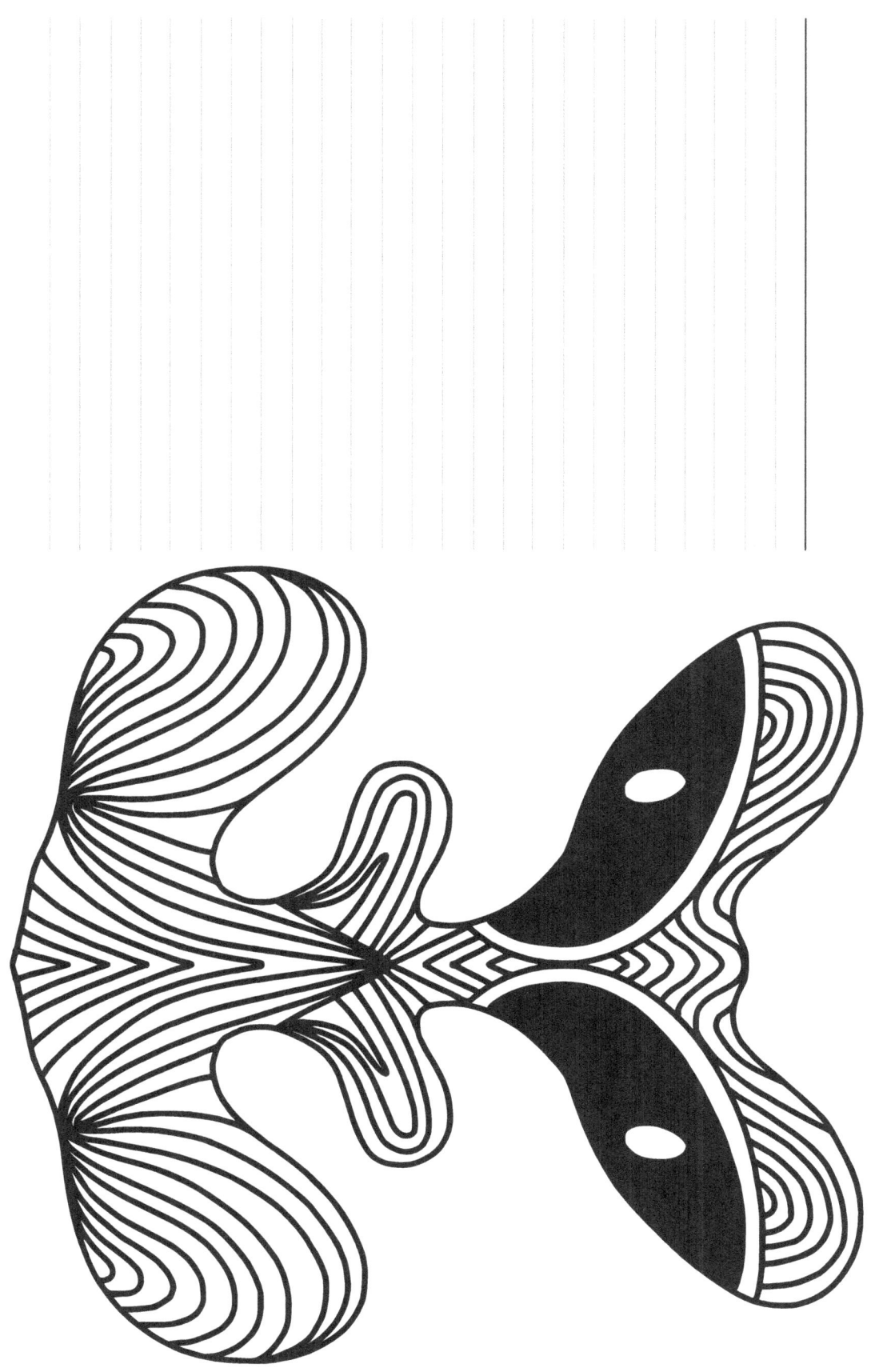

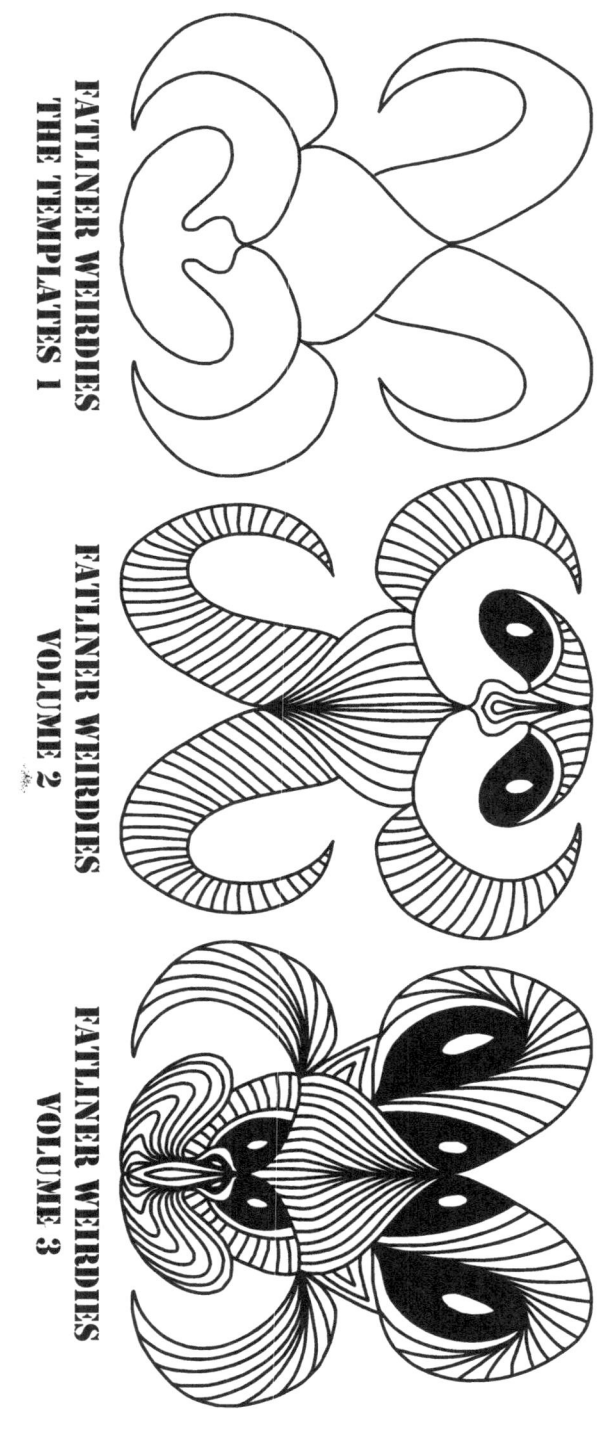

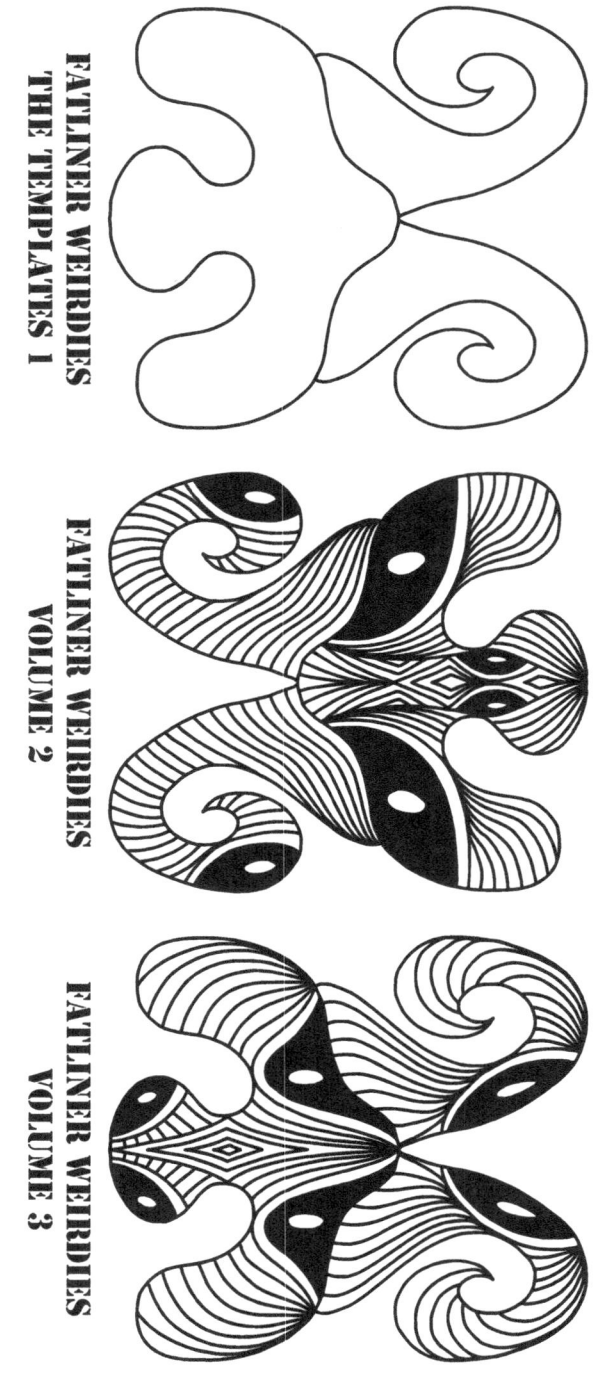

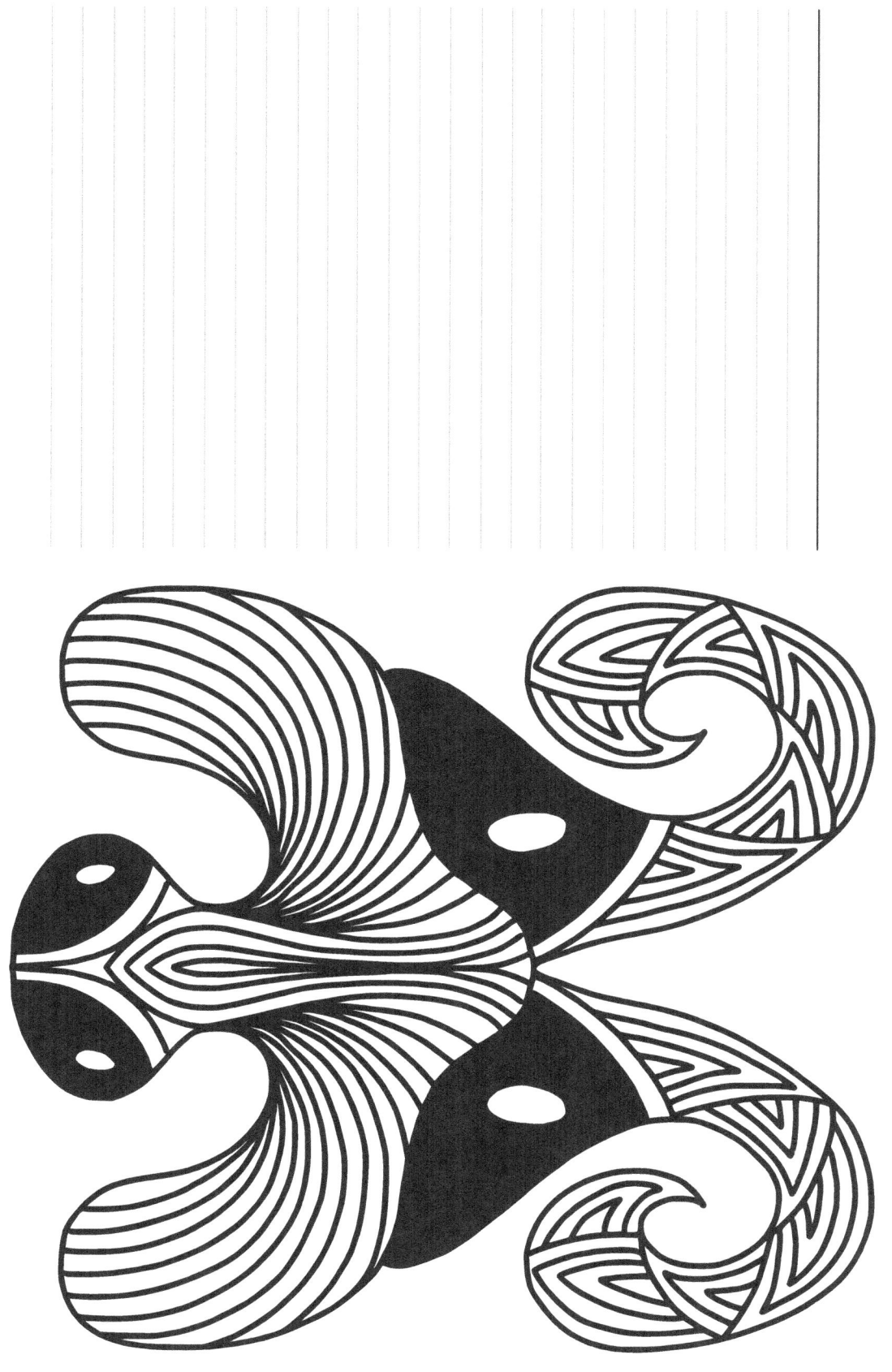

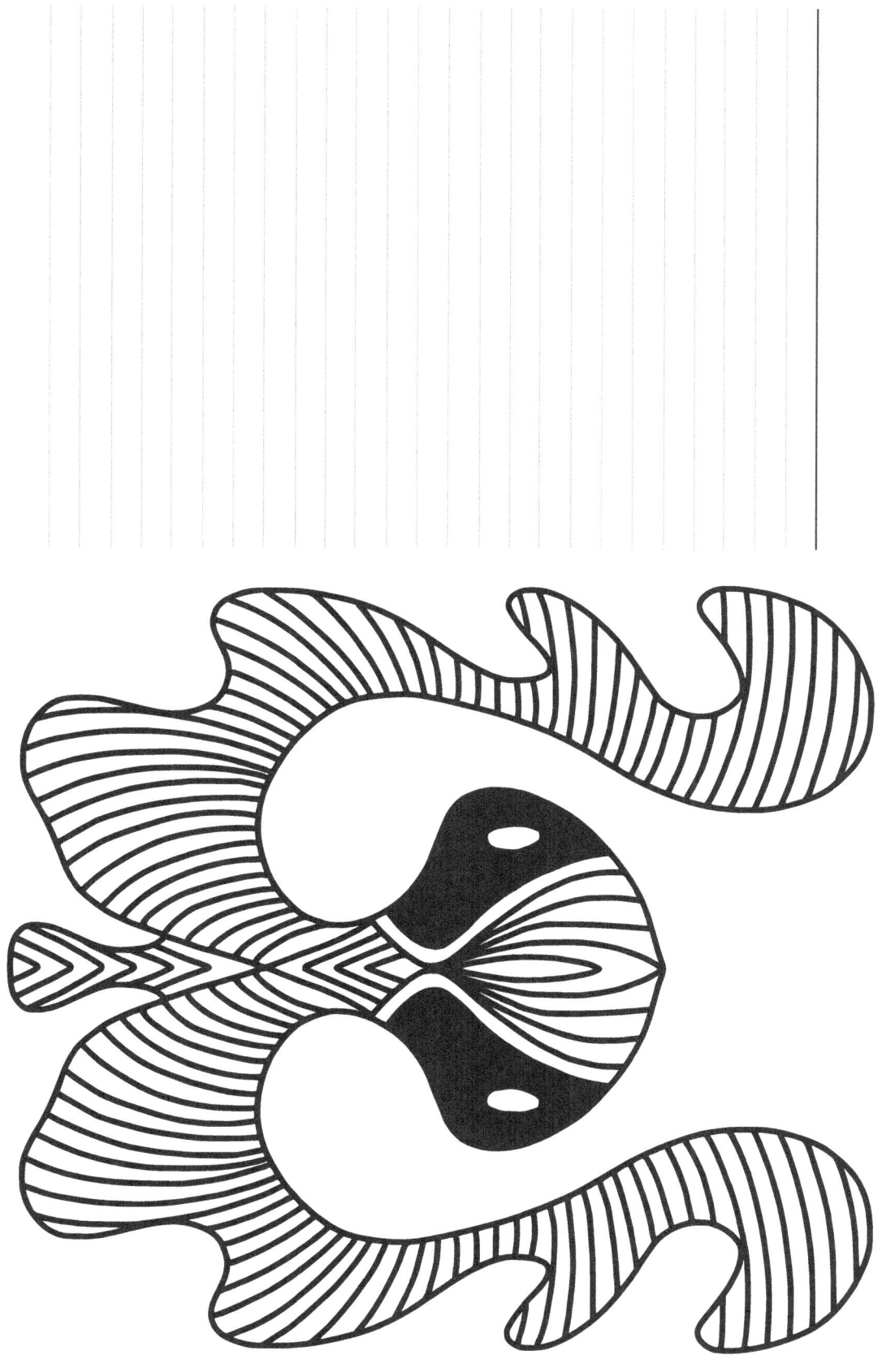

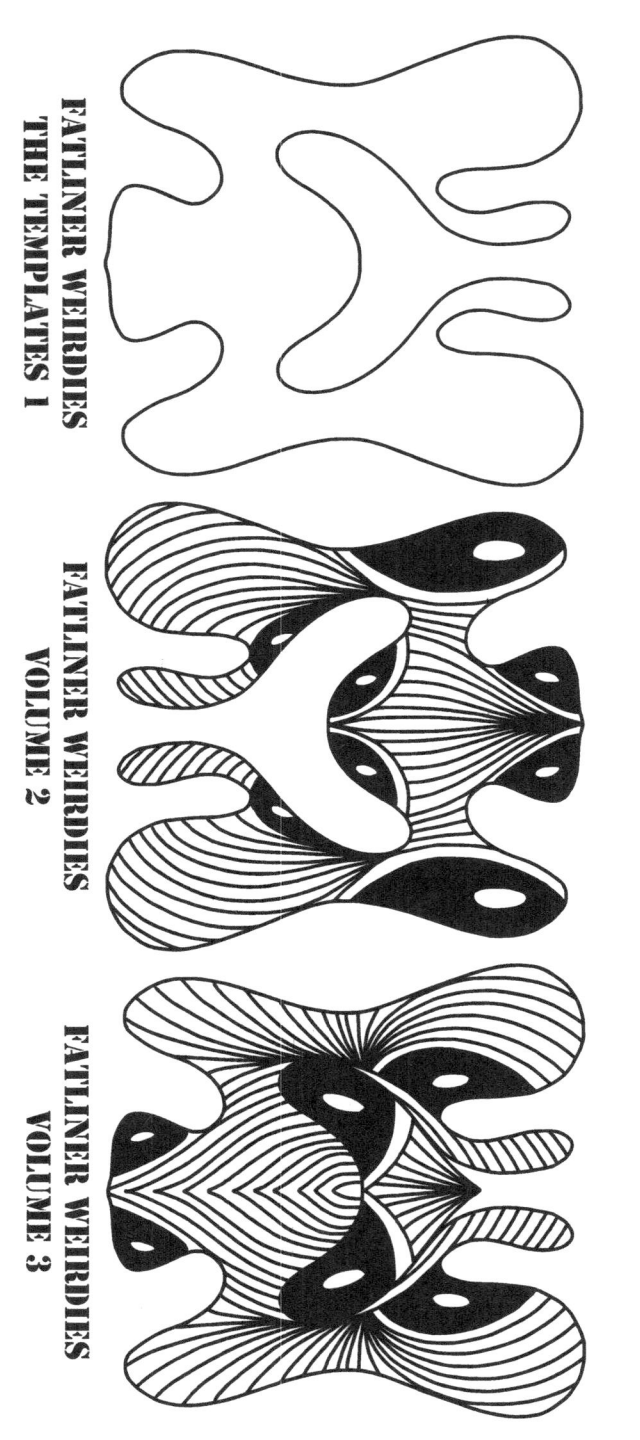

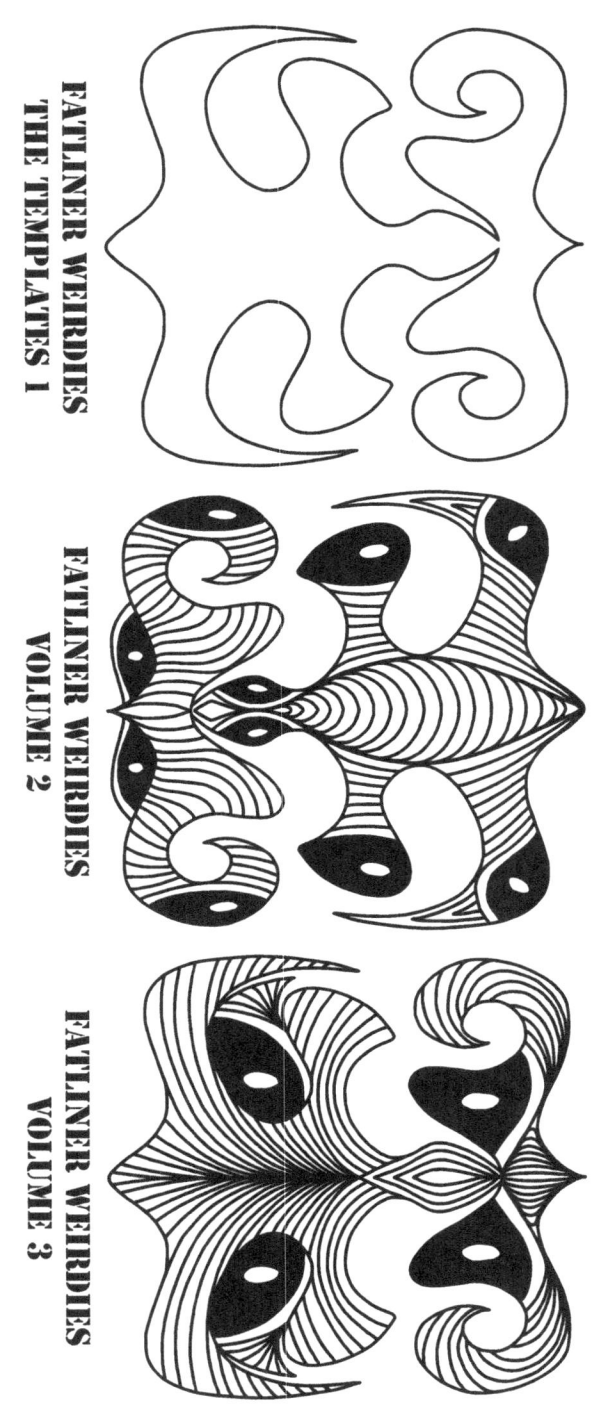

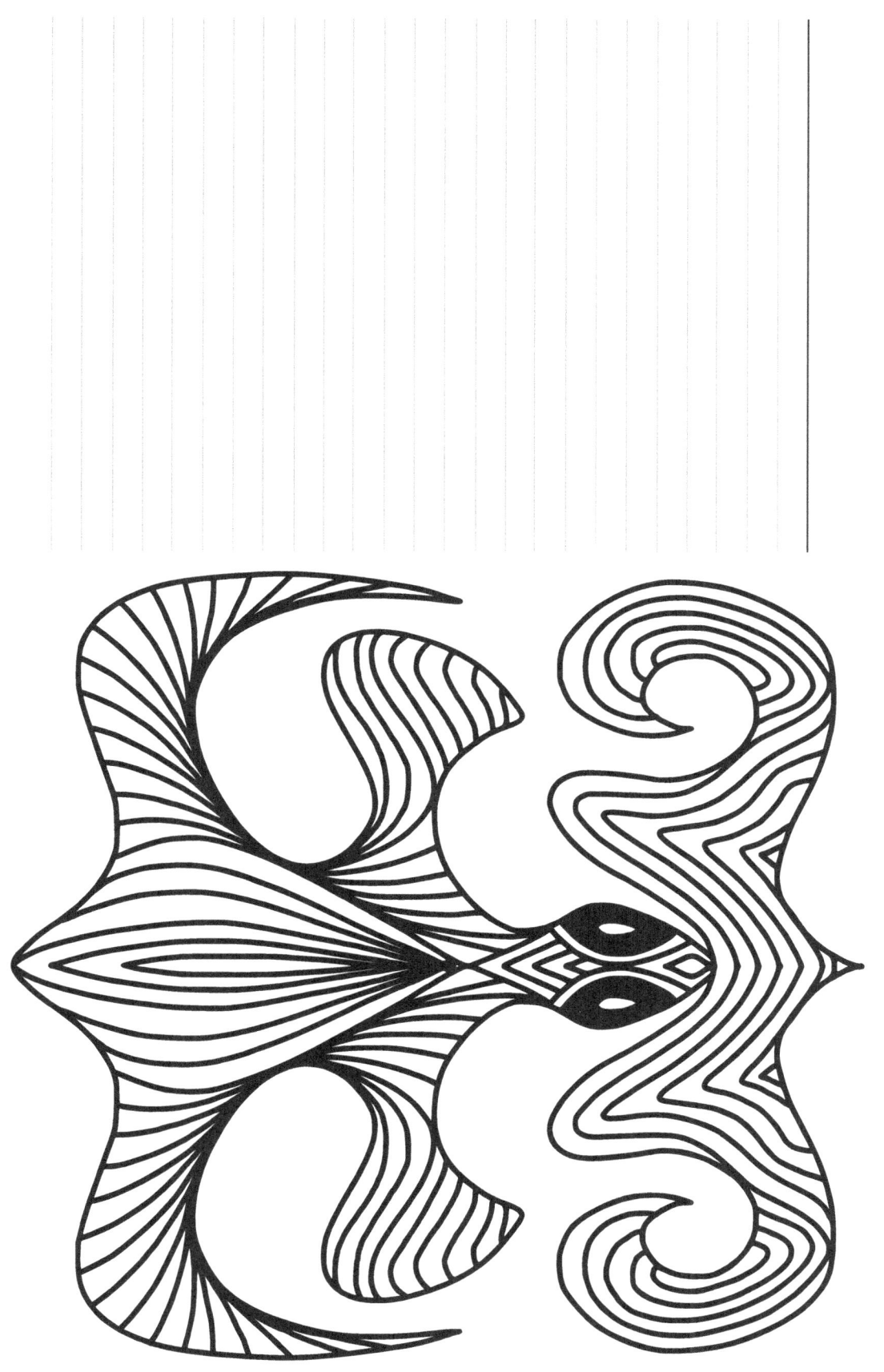

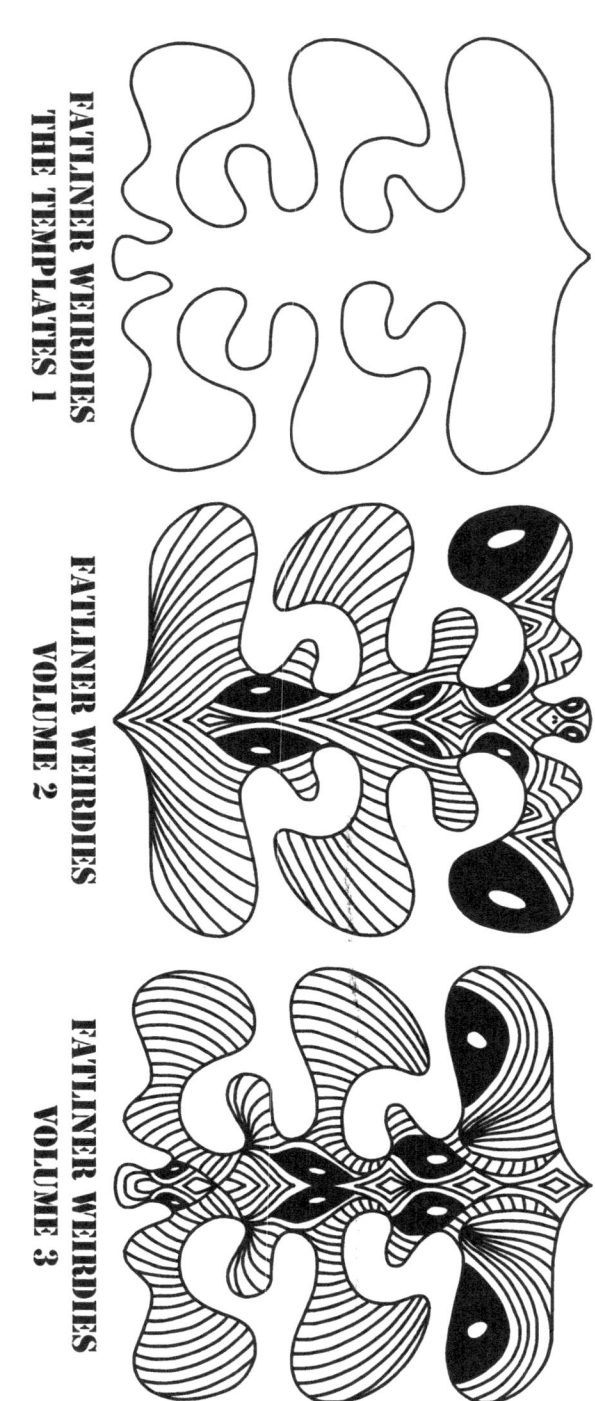

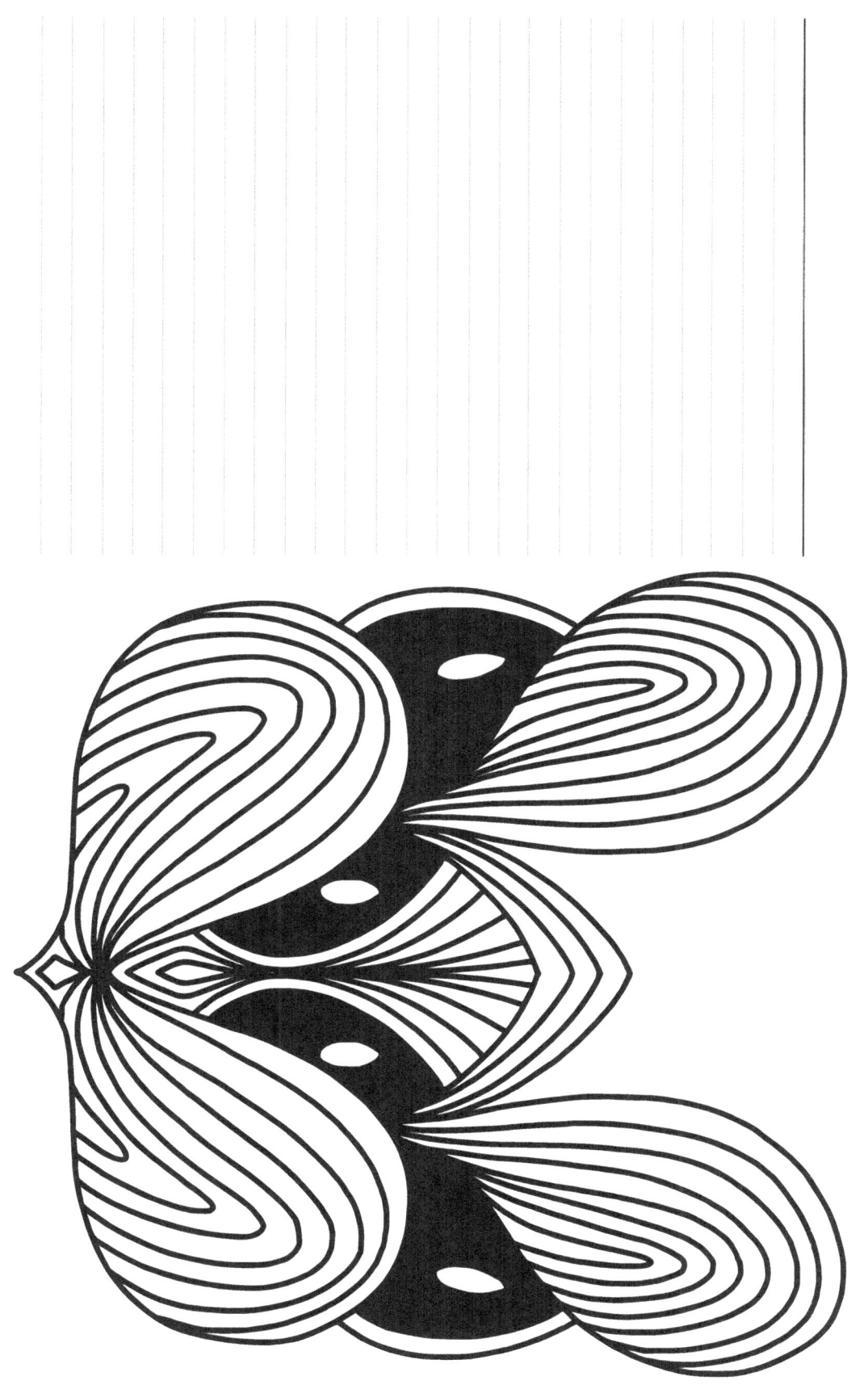